Redemption™
Player's Guide

David M. Easterling

Foreword by Douglas H. Gresham
Author of LENTEN LANDS: My Childhood with
Joy Davidman and C.S. Lewis

© 1996 Cactus Game Design, Inc.

All rights reserved.

1553 Military Highway
Chesapeake, VA 23320

Printed in the United States of America

Redemption™ is a trademark of Cactus Game Design, Inc.

Cover Illustration by Jeff Haynie

Library of Congress Cataloging-in-Publication Data

Easterling, David M. 1959-
Redemption™ Player's Guide / by David M. Easterling
p. 192
Includes Index
Includes Glossary
1. Bible games and puzzles 2. Redemption™ (Game)
3. Card games–rules
I. David M. Easterling
II. Title
ISBN 1-889055-04-2
Library of Congress Catalog Card Number: 96-86523

Unless otherwise marked, Scripture quotations are from the King James version of the Bible.

First Printing, November 1996

Welcome to the Redemption™ Player's Guide

Redemption™ is a collectable trading card game of Biblical adventures for two or more players. You lead your brave band of Heroes in a series of encounters against the evil forces of your opponents. The object of the game is to be the first to rescue five Lost Souls who are being held prisoner in the Land of Bondage.

The Redemption™ Player's Guide will help you build superior play decks and give you hints about strategy to surprise all your friends.

Redemption™ Mission Statement

Games are wonderful tools for bringing people together for fun and fellowship. This is our goal with Redemption™. We have tried to create a game that is both entertaining and edifying. We want you, the players, to have a wonderful time.

Part of the enjoyment associated with the game lies in custom-building your own deck prior to play. Players continually discover new strategies for creating the "unbeatable" deck, but they need specific cards to fit these strategies. Trading allows you to obtain cards that will fill weak spots in your deck. There are many different cards: common, uncommon and rare which may be acquired in booster packs or by trading to build competitive decks.

All of the concepts for the cards come from the Bible. We have tried to give the best Scriptural reference whenever possible and practical. Some concepts in the game are spread out over multiple chapters in the Bible and cannot be printed on a single card. If a card creates a question in your mind, look it up in the Bible and read the relevant verse within the context given in Scripture. We have tried to be Biblically accurate. If you find a mistake, write and let me know.

Have fun, and happy gaming!
— **Rob Anderson,**
President, **Cactus Game Design, Inc.**
Redemption™ Game creator & designer

MEET THE AUTHOR

David M. Easterling is a graduate of Lexington Theological Seminary. He is a 15 year veteran of youth ministry and is an author, editor, event speaker, workshop leader, and musician. David is the president of SongWeaver Resources, Inc., the editor of the *CMC UPDATE* and *The Jesus FanZine*. He has written for many Christian resources including *LinC, Questions Senior Highs Ask*, and *CONNECT*, as well as *Youth!, Parents Living with Teenagers, Alive Now, Devo'Zine, Leader* and other magazines.

David is a long-time fan of adventure and strategy games. He and Laurie, his wife, enjoy reading, games, spending time with family, writing, concerts, science fiction, retreats, the mountains, and mountain top experiences.

David's E-mail address is 76713.113@compuserve.com. Please send him a note telling what you like best about *Redemption*™ and this book.

Other books by David Easterling:
Confronting Fear (in the *YouthSearch* series)
Genesis, Part Two (in the *By The Book* series)
Forgiveness is Forever: New Parables and Psalms for Our Spiritual Journey

Other books edited by David Easterling:
United Methodist Youth Program Annual, Vol. 3
United Methodist Youth Mission and Events Annual, Vol. 3

TABLE OF CONTENTS

ACKNOWLEDGMENTS

Redemption™ Player's Guide production team:

Editor/Author:	David M. Easterling
Associate Editor:	Robert J. Anderson
Production Editor:	Rodger "Tim" Moloney
Copy Editors:	Laurie C. Easterling
	Hal Casey
Graphic Designer:	Cheryl Krasucki
Cover Art:	Jeff Haynie

David M. Easterling, author and editor of the *Redemption*™ Player's Guide, would like to thank:

Rob Anderson, for his friendship, gift of caring, designing a wonderful game and asking me to write this book.

Laurie Easterling, my wife, for her many insights, hours of proofreading, sample game she created, and 13 years of love and caring.

My family: Dad, Mom, Del, Larry, and Sarah, for all the fun times growing up; playing board games and card games—especially Rook®.

The 50,000 people who are playing *Redemption*™ and have asked for a player's guide. You are the ultimate play testers!

The many play testers who have responded with ideas and feedback about several sections in this book. They include: Rodney Barnes, Ira Cole, John J. Coleman, Craig "C-dog" Evans, Carl Forhan, R. Craig Haines, Robert J. Howell, John Jackson, Marcus Johnson, Steven Jones, Michael Lane, Brent Siefken, Mike "Quaff" Thornton, Dave Townley, Robert A. Warren, Chris West, Davis Willey, and the players in the Fellowship of the Redeemed (Stuart, Trina and Todd Whitaker, Lichiel Critchfield, Shawn and Ben Parrish).

The God Most High—who cares about people enough to love us, walk with us, and save us—the lost, the last, the least, and the lonely. This is the ultimate good news of redemption.

ACKNOWLEDGMENTS

Rob Anderson, the designer & creator of the *Redemption*™ Card Game, would like to thank:

David Easterling, a new found friend, brother, and rules lawyer for a job well done on this book.

My wife Susan, for too many things to list.

Players of *Redemption*™, for their support, ideas and friendships.

To my children: Paul, Scott, Mark and Danika, for the blessing they send me to work with every morning, "Good-bye Dad. Have a good day. Walk in the Spirit."

To the people I work with at Cactus, Pete, Tim, Troy and Bette, for believing in me and this game and putting everything on the line to publish this game.

To God, the Master and Creator of the Universe, for creating us in his image. It is God given imagination and creativity that allows us to create games like *Redemption*™.

FOREWORD

When I was growing up in England I spent most of my time playing outside. We did not have a television in the house for entertainment (and smart people, in their right mind, would probably still not have one in their house today). But since our family was a reading family and there were thousands of books in the house, I read all the time.

Sometimes we would play board games. I remember playing chess, *Monopoly*® and especially *Scrabble*®. Of course, none of us, not even Warnie, would play with the special "house rules" with which mother (Joy Davidman) and Jack (C. S. Lewis) played. They would combine the letters of two *Scrabble*® games and then allow words from all known languages, both real and fictitious, as long as you could provide the "chapter and verse" evidence that the word you had used really did exist.

Games can provide us with some wonderful childhood memories and can be instrumental in developing our social skills by teaching us how to relate with other people. Games stimulate our imaginations, and hone our intellectual abilities.

Redemption™ seems to me to have some very real benefits over and above those other games. Gaming has become a pastime of many people throughout society and as such has become a target area for corruption and evil influence. *Redemption*™ turns this around and introduces an awareness of spiritual warfare into the minds of players, a vital awareness that we need to recapture. The evil one has for a long time tried to blind us to what he is really doing to our society and keep us unaware of his machinations. With this game, one becomes aware of his schemes.

Redemption™ also brings to mind the value of the words of Scripture. We desperately need to take back from Satan those parts of our society in which he is most active. The communications media, the political arena, and our pastimes and leisure activities. *Redemption*™ is a first and important step along this vital road. As you play the game, realize that what you do in the Field of Battle in play, you can do in the Field of Battle in real life.

Redemption™ can be a training ground for the real war against evil in our own lives.

Douglas H. Gresham
County Carlow, Ireland

Redemption™

Player's Guide

David M. Easterling

INTRODUCTION

Editor's Note: I went to Atlanta Fest during June of 1996. I remember that it is was extremely hot—almost 100 degrees in the shade. I went to listen to some great Christian music and visit with some of the musicians I knew. Another reason I drove to Atlanta was to interview Rob Anderson about the *Redemption*™ Card Game for an article to be printed in **The Jesus FanZine**. When we were talking during lunch, Rob asked me if I would consider writing a player's guide for the game to help answer the many questions they were getting. I had already become extremely fond of the game and had been playing it for several months; so I jumped at the chance to write this book.

During the summer of 1993, Rob Anderson received a call at Cactus from Darwin Bromley of **Mayfair Games**. Darwin suggested that Rob should check into the new collectable card game (CCG) phenomena that might just open up a whole new game category. There were two innovative key factors to CCGs. One was that cards were sold in starter decks and booster packs containing rare, uncommon, and common cards which were randomly sorted. The other key was that players could customize or build their play decks with whatever cards they liked best. The various cards would allow players to take different actions to affect the game depending upon the way the cards were played.

During the next year, Rob developed several CCG proposals and submitted them to game publishers. All were turned down. During a much needed family vacation to Florida, the inspiration for a game based upon the Bible began to develop in Rob's mind. Rob created some card ideas and began playtesting the early version of the game which would become *Redemption*™. Rob tried for several months to persuade game companies to produce the game, but no one would take a risk on a CCG based upon the Bible.

Rob decided that this game had the potential to not only be fun for fellowship, but also could be an important tool for education and evangelism. He decided to raise capital, hire freelance artists, and assign all the in-house duties needed to convert from a game design company into a game publishing company. In Mid-1995, *Redemption*™ was released to encouraging reviews and responses from both the Christian market and the mainstream adventure game market. The game was previewed at the *Christian Booksellers Association* convention and orders began coming in.

When developing artwork for the cards, great care was given to reflect the nature of persons and events described in the Scriptural text of the card. Since some of the cards illustrate the evil actions of people in the Bible, some parents might feel that the illustrations on certain cards are inappropriate for their children. **Cactus Game Design, Inc.** supports parental decisions in this matter. Anyone who returns a card for this reason, will receive an alternate card to replace it. The game does not depend on any individual card and it will continue to play well when some of the cards are removed.

Cactus Game Design, Inc. has sold thousands of starter decks. In fact, over 18 million cards have now been sold. The Prophets expansion set has been enthusiastically embraced by players because of the exceptional diversity of the characters and special ability cards. Players have been excitedly E-mailing each other with great card combinations for game play. Several web sites feature information about the game. The official *Redemption™* web site is:

http://www/redemption.com/

Players are now eagerly awaiting the next expansion set.

Redemption™ Fellowship Tournaments are being sponsored every week across the country in Christian bookstores, churches, game retailers, malls, and homes. Youth and young adults are using the cards to introduce their friends to the people and stories of the Bible. Players are learning things they had never realized were in the Bible. For some people this clever game has rekindled an interest in Bible study. *Redemption™* is having a profound effect upon people and is living up to its name as people are finding faith in God through the caring fellowship of friends.

In writing this player's guide to answer the many questions that players were asking about how cards could be played, Rob and I discovered that the uses of some cards had been overlooked, and the common usage of other cards was not quite "legal" according to the rules and the exact wording of special abilities on the cards. In this guide you will find that the rules have been expanded and rewritten in great detail. Special attention has been given to timing and card abilities. Most of the questions you may have had will be answered in these pages. Some of the new rulings are different from play in the past, constituting alteration of a few previous rulings on card play.

The *Redemption*™ Player's Guide is the official way the game should be played, especially considering the many players who will be meeting for the first time to play in tournaments. Our intention is not to tell anyone that they have been playing the game incorrectly. The real value of this guide is that players from anywhere in the country can sit down together and play by the same rules and understand the results of the game play in the same way. If your group decides to play by "house rules," no "*Redemption*™ Rules Lawyers" will knock down your door and make you feel guilty. This is a game and it is supposed to be fun as well as challenging.

By placing the cards into new categories and introducing players to new ways of playing and thinking about the game, we know that new questions and play combinations will be discovered that were never noticed before. There just might be enough new ideas for another book after more expansion sets are released.

Tell us your discoveries about game play. Please send in the player's survey or write a letter. The staff at **Cactus Game Design, Inc.** enjoy hearing from players.

Our prayer is that by reading this book you will learn of the many wonderful ways that *Redemption*™ can be played and that this game will be a blessing to you and your friends.

GLOSSARY

The Glossary is inserted here because it is necessary to become familiar with the game terms and their definitions in order to understand how to play this game. Basic definitions are included in this section, and many terms are explained in greater detail in other sections.

Army of God: The Army of God is composed of Heroes and is identified by the Cross in the icon box located in the upper left corner of each card.

Banding: When an enhancement card that allows banding is played, two or more characters join together in the field of battle and are treated as a combined force for dealing and receiving damage. Heroes may only band with Heroes. Evil Characters may only band with Evil Characters.

Battle Challenge: When there is not a Lost Soul available to rescue, a player may issue a Battle Challenge to the opposing player. The Battle Challenge is initiated by placing a Hero into the field of battle and inviting the opposing player to place an Evil Character into the field of battle to meet the challenge. The opposing player may decide not to risk losing any cards by simply not sending an Evil Character into the field of battle. If the challenge is not met, no enhancement cards can be played with that Hero while it is in the field of battle because the losing character plays the first enhancement and a Hero alone in the field of battle cannot be losing. The Hero would then be returned to the owner's territory. If the opposing player decides to accept the challenge and places an Evil Character into the field of battle, both players would be able to add enhancement cards in the same way as in a rescue attempt during the battle phase.

Bible Icon Card: A Bible icon card is a good enhancement card used to increase the offensive strength and defensive toughness of a Hero. These cards are identified by the Bible in the icon box located in the upper left corner of each card. The good enhancement card must have the same color in the icon box as the Hero with which it is to be played. Many of these enhancement cards also contain specific instructions (special abilities) which affect the game play.

Block: Evil Characters are played in the field of battle to try to block or prevent a rescue. Only one Evil Character may block during a turn unless a banding enhancement card, such as **Rage**, is played to allow two Evil Character cards to block on the same turn.

Brigade: A brigade is a subgroup of either the Army of God or the evil forces and is identified by the color of the icon box in the upper left corner of the card.

Character Abilities: The strength of a character is represented by the numbers, such as 6/6, within the colored icon box. The first number is the offensive strength and the second number is the defensive toughness. A character's offensive strength is the number of points of damage done to an opposing character in the field of battle. A character card is defeated and discarded at the end of the turn when it receives enough points of damage equal to or greater than its defensive toughness.

Character Card: The three basic types of character cards in the game of *Redemption™* are Heroes, Evil Characters, and Lost Souls.

Color (of Brigade): The color of the icon box in the upper left corner of the card determines in which color brigade a card belongs. The Heroes and the Evil Characters are each divided into 6 different color brigades.

Counters: Counters, such as milk caps, coins, dice, or paper clips, are used to keep track of which Lost Soul cards belong to which players and are especially useful in a multi-player game. Counters are also used for keeping track of the number of rounds a character is set aside, and for designating the new abilities of a character once it is returned to play from the set-aside area.

Cross Icon Card: A cross in the icon box located in the upper left corner of the card indicates that the card is a Hero.

Damage: Damage is dealt to a character by an opposing character's strength. Enough damage is done to defeat a character when that character's defensive toughness ends up at 0 or less. Damage is simultaneously totaled for characters at the end of the Battle Phase when the players decide not to add any more cards to the battle. *Note: The exceptions are cards that cause damage until the end of turn, and first-strike enhancement cards.*

Deck: A play deck is composed of the cards a player chooses to use in the game. When a player uses a deck different from the basic A or B deck which comes in the dual starter set, then that player has what is commonly referred to as a customized, theme, or tuned deck.

Defeat: A character card is defeated and discarded at the end of the turn if it receives points of damage equal to or greater than its defensive toughness.

Discard: Discarding is the action of sending a card to be placed onto the top of the discard pile. A card might be discarded from a player's hand, draw deck, or field of play. Once a card is discarded it cannot be re-introduced to game play unless another card's special instructions allow this to happen.

Dragon Icon Card: A dragon in the icon box indicates that the card is an Evil Character.

Enhancement Card: An enhancement card is often used to increase the strength and toughness of the Heroes or Evil Characters of matching color brigades which are in the field of battle. Many enhancement cards also contain specific instructions (special abilities) which affect the game play. The special abilities are activated by playing the enhancement card with a character of the same color brigade in the field of battle. Most enhancement cards are immediately discarded when a battle is over. Set-aside enhancement cards may be used with any appropriate character in the field of play.

Evil Character: The Evil Characters guard the Lost Souls in a player's Land of Bondage and are used to block rescue attempts from other players.

Evil Forces: The evil forces are composed of Evil Characters identified by the dragon icon located in the upper left corner of the card.

Field of Battle: This is the area in the field of play where Heroes and Evil Characters meet in battle during a rescue attempt or battle challenge.

Field of Play: The field of play includes all the cards from all players that are on the playing surface except for draw piles, discard piles, set-aside areas, and Redeemed Souls in the Land of Redemption. It does not include the cards which are in the players' hands.

First-Strike Ability: An enhancement card with this ability played with a character in the field of battle allows the character to survive when a battle ends in what would ordinarily be a mutual destruction situation. Normally, damage is dealt simultaneously, but a character with the first-strike ability actually deals all damage first before the opposing character returns any damage; thus only the opposing character is defeated and discarded. If both players have played a first-strike card, then because of the timing rules, the player who played first-strike first, would win in a mutual destruction situation because the opposing character would already be defeated and discarded before the second first-strike card could take effect.

Grim Reaper Icon Card: These instant cards can be played whenever desired by the holder, even when it is not his or her turn. The ability of each of these powerful cards is stated on the card. A deck may contain only one of each of these cards. *Example: One **Christian Martyr** and one **Burial** may be in the same deck, but only one of each.*

Healing: A healing card will save a Hero which is either "about to be" or "is being discarded" depending upon the special ability of the individual card. A Hero that has been healed may not return to the field of battle during that same turn.

Hero: Heroes are the characters in the Army of God. They try to rescue Lost Souls by battling Evil Characters in the field of battle during rescue attempts.

Ignore: When an enhancement card having the "ignore" special ability is played with a Hero, that Hero cannot take any direct damage, be directly affected, or be defeated by any Evil Character or enhancement from the color brigade or card type specified on the "ignore" enhancement. The Hero successfully wins the rescue attempt unless the opponent can play an enhancement card (such as **Rage** or **Ram with Two Horns**) which would introduce an Evil Character from a different color brigade into the battle, to continue blocking the Hero. A player may still play enhancement cards with an Evil Character from a color brigade that a Hero is ignoring in order to affect other characters in play.

Immediate Effect: Some enhancement cards have an immediate effect the moment they are played and do not allow an opposing player the chance to prevent that effect. Cards such as **Authority of Christ**, **Chains**, **False Peace**, **Baggage** and **Net** have immediate effects. Cards having an immediate effect on game play are often referred to as winners or stoppers.

In Play: Any card that is in the field of play is considered to be in play.

Instant Card: An instant card is one of the specialty cards which has a Lamb or Grim Reaper icon symbol in the top left corner. The special ability of an instant card takes effect when played and does not allow an opponent to prevent that effect.

Lamb Icon Card: These instant cards can be played whenever desired by the holder, even when it is not his turn. The special ability of each of these powerful cards is stated on the card. A deck may contain only one of each of these cards. *Example: One **Son of God** card and one **Angel of the Lord** card may be in the same deck, but only one of each.*

Land of Bondage: The Land of Bondage is the area where Lost Souls and captured prisoners are held.

Land of Redemption: The Land of Redemption is the area of sanctuary where rescued souls (Redeemed Souls) and rescued Heroes reside during a game.

Lost Soul: Lost Souls are characters that are being held prisoner by the evil forces in the Land of Bondage. Once a Lost Soul character is rescued, it is no longer a Lost Soul; it is now a Redeemed Soul.

Mutual Destruction: A mutual destruction situation occurs during a rescue attempt when the total offensive strength of the Hero is greater than or equal to the total defensive toughness of the Evil Character, **and** the total offensive strength of the Evil Character is greater than or equal to the total defensive toughness of the Hero. When this happens and neither player can play any more cards to change the situation, then both characters are discarded. The rescue attempt is still successful, because any Hero would sacrifice his or her own life to rescue a Lost Soul. If a card with the first-strike ability has been played, then only the opposing character is discarded.

Pass: In a stalemate or mutual destruction situation a player may pass the initiative to allow the opponent the choice of playing the next enhancement card. If the opponent passes back to the other player, then that player must play next or else not play any more enhancement cards during that turn. The opponent then has one more chance to play before the battle is resolved. When a player is no longer in a stalemate or mutual destruction situation, passing the initiative is not allowed.

Power Enhancement Card: Some enhancement cards are not limited to being played with one color brigade. These cards are identified by their multi-colored icon box and are sometimes referred to by players as rainbow cards. Power enhancement cards may be played to increase the strength and toughness of any character card (of the appropriate army in the field of battle) from any color brigade. Each deck may contain only one of each multi-colored card. *Example: A deck may contain* **Sword of the Spirit, Shoes of Peace,** *and* **Sun Worship,** *but only one of each card.*

Repel: When an enhancement card having the "repel" special ability is played with an Evil Character, that Evil Character cannot take any direct damage, be directly affected or be defeated by any Hero or enhancement from the color brigade or card type specified on the repel enhancement card. The Evil Character successfully blocks the rescue attempt unless the rescuer can play a banding enhancement card (such as **Sound the Alarm** or **Ezekiel's Stick**) which would introduce into the battle a Hero from a different color brigade or card type to continue the rescue attempt. A player may still play enhancement cards with a Hero from a color brigade or card type that an Evil Character is repelling in order to affect other characters in play.

Rescue: The blocking Evil Character(s) in the field of battle must be absent, defeated, ignored, converted, captured, discarded, or otherwise removed from the field of battle for a rescue attempt to be successful.

Rescue Attempt: A rescue attempt begins when a Hero tries to rescue a Lost Soul. A player may only make one rescue attempt per turn by sending one Hero into the field of battle to attempt the rescue. Only one Hero is allowed in the field of battle during a rescue attempt, unless a banding card (such as **Sound the Alarm**) is played.

Set-Aside Card: Enhancement cards with the set-aside special ability allow a character to increase in strength for each turn in which the character card remains set aside from the field of play. A character which is set aside is out of play and cannot be affected by other cards. Character cards may not be used while in the set-aside area, nor may other enhancement cards be played on them since they are out of the field of play. The set-aside character must be brought back into the player's territory during that player's turn in order to be used again in the field of play. When a character card is brought back into play, the set-aside enhancement card is immediately discarded, but the character remains at the new levels of strength and toughness until it is defeated or the game ends. Use counters to keep track of the number of turns that characters are set aside.

Skull Icon Card: A skull icon card is an evil enhancement card used to increase the offensive strength and defensive toughness of an Evil Character. These cards are identified by the skull in the icon box located in the upper left corner of each card. An evil enhancement card must have the same color in the icon box as the Evil Character with which it is to be played. Many of these enhancement cards also contain specific instructions (special abilities) which affect the game play.

Specialty Card: Specialty cards are identified by either the Lamb icon or the Grim Reaper icon located in the upper left corner of the card. A specialty card can be played whenever desired by the holder. The special abilities of the card take effect immediately. A deck may contain only one of each individual specialty card.

Stalemate: A stalemate occurs when neither character in the field of battle is doing enough damage to the opposing character to cause that character to be discarded. When the Battle Phase ends with a stalemate, the rescue attempt is unsuccessful, the Lost Soul remains in the Land of Bondage, both characters are returned to their territories, and the enhancements that were played are discarded. *Example: The Hero is 14/18 and the Evil Character is 15/16 and neither player can add any more cards. When the damage is added up, the Hero's defensive toughness is still at +3 and the Evil Character's defensive toughness is at +2.*

Strength: Strength, the offensive ability of a character; the first number in the icon box.

Territory: The player's territory is the area within the field of play where a player places the Lost Soul, Evil Character, and Hero cards. A player's territory does not include the field of battle, the set-aside area, draw pile, discard pile, Land of Redemption, or the player's hand.

Tie: A tie happens when both characters are discarded (mutual destruction) or neither character is discarded (stalemate).

Timing: The timing of when cards are played is important. Players will discover that the same cards may yield different outcomes if they are played in a different order. Keep track of the order in which cards are played so that battle can be accurately resolved.

Toughness: Toughness, the defensive ability of a character; the second number in the icon box.

Turn: A player's turn begins with the draw phase and ends at the end of the discard phase when a player announces he is finished.

THE ANATOMY OF A CARD

Character Card

Character abilities
(offense/defense)

Card Icon and
brigade color

Name of card

Illustration

Biblical text

Biblical reference

Artist

Enhancement Card

Name of card

Card Icon and
brigade color

Illustration

Special Ability

Biblical text

Biblical reference

Artist

RECOMMENDED CARD ARRANGEMENT

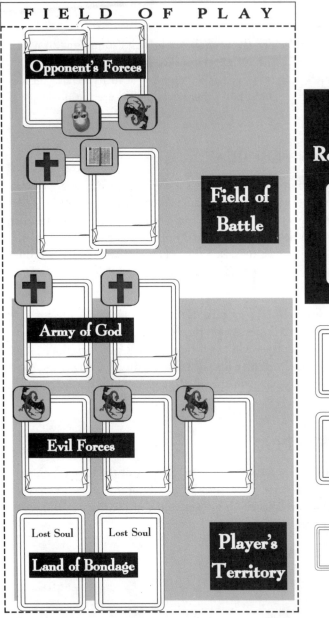

BASIC GAME RULES

EQUIPMENT

Each player will need a deck of *Redemption*™ cards and something to use as counters (milk caps, coins, dice, or paper clips) to help keep track of which cards belong to which players, as well as the number of turns a character has been set aside. Soft drinks, chips, and other refreshments are optional.

PREPARATION FOR PLAY

Decks must contain a minimum of 50 cards including seven Lost Soul cards. For every seven cards beyond 50, one of those seven must be a Lost Soul. A deck of 56 cards contains only seven Lost Souls, while a deck of 57 must contain eight Lost Souls. A deck of 57-63 cards contains eight Lost Souls, while a deck of 64-70 cards contains nine Lost Souls. (The rare **Lost Souls** card only counts as one card and one Lost Soul for deck construction and is limited to only one for each 50 cards in your deck.)

Players thoroughly shuffle their own card decks. Players may ask to shuffle an opponent's deck as well. Each player will then cut the deck of the opponent. In a multi-player game each player will cut the deck of the player to the left. Determine the player who will play first by rolling a die, drawing straws, tossing a coin, or playing rock-scissors-paper. Let the games begin!

SEQUENCE OF PLAY

During a player's turn there are several phases or steps of the turn which may occur. Players will always draw three cards at the beginning of their turn (except the opening round) and reduce down to eight cards in their hands, if necessary, when ending their turns.

Draw Phase
(Draw cards to add to hand)

Upkeep Phase
(Change counters if necessary)

Action Phase
(Choose one or more of the following actions)
    a. Play Characters into the field of play.
    b. Declare a rescue attempt or battle challenge.
    c. Play an instant card.
    d. Set aside a character or return a character from the set-aside area to the field of play.
    e. Go to discard phase.

Battle Phase
(Resolve a rescue attempt or battle challenge)

Discard Phase
(Ends the player's turn)

Draw Phase

At the beginning of the game each player draws eight cards from the top of his own draw pile to form a starting hand. Every time a player draws a Lost Soul card it is immediately placed in that player's Land of Bondage and another card is drawn to replace it in his hand.

Players always draw cards from the top of their own decks and may not look at any other cards in their decks once play begins until the cards are drawn normally at the beginning of the player's turn. The only exception is when a special ability card allows a player to scan a deck and remove a card, but a deck is always reshuffled when this occurs.

At the beginning of each player's second turn, and each turn thereafter, three cards are drawn. Each time a Lost Soul is drawn it is immediately placed in that player's Land of Bondage and one replacement card is drawn.

Upkeep Phase

As soon as you have drawn three cards to begin a turn, you should make any upkeep changes which might be necessary. This would include adding a counter to set-aside characters, returning set-aside characters to your territory, or adjusting a character's abilities.

Action Phase

Although the "action phase" terminology may be new to some players, the same choices are available during this phase. You may make one or more of the following choices. (Returning a character from a set-aside area is not an option on the first turn.)

a) Place any Heroes or Evil Characters into your territory, but no duplicate character cards are allowed in play in your territory. *Example: You may have more than one Mary in your deck or hand, but only one Mary may be in your territory at a time.*

b) Declare a rescue attempt or battle challenge by placing a Hero in the field of battle. You may challenge your opponent by making a rescue attempt if there is a Lost Soul available or by making a battle challenge when there is not a Lost Soul available in your opponent's Land of Bondage. When this action is taken the battle phase begins to resolve the rescue attempt or battle challenge.

c) Play a Specialty card, which immediately takes effect according to the instructions on the card.

d) Set aside a Hero or return a Hero from a set-aside area to your territory in the field of play. Set aside an Evil Character or return an Evil Character from a set-aside area to your territory in the field of play.

e) Go directly to the discard phase to end your turn.

Battle Phase

When a Hero and an Evil Character meet in the field of battle, you will follow this sequence of events to determine the result of the battle.

1) If you declared that you are making a rescue attempt or battle challenge during the action phase, then you have placed one Hero into the field of battle. The Hero may be played from your hand or territory. (Only one Hero may be used in a rescue attempt unless a banding enhancement card is later played allowing an additional Hero to join in the rescue attempt.) Players are only allowed to make one rescue attempt (or battle challenge) per turn. A Battle Challenge is resolved in the same way as a rescue attempt, except the player will not win a Lost Soul, because there is not one available.

2) If the opponent being attacked chooses to block, then an Evil Character from that player's hand or territory is placed in the field of battle as the blocking card. (Only one Evil Character may be used to block the rescue attempt unless a banding enhancement card is later played with the blocker. Banding allows another Evil Character to enter the field of battle and join in blocking the rescue attempt.)

3) If the opponent does not block your rescue attempt, you win a Lost Soul. If your opponent does not block your Battle Challenge, the Hero would then be returned to your territory and no enhancement cards could be played with that Hero (because the player of the losing character plays the next enhancement, and a Hero alone in the field of battle cannot be losing).

4) If at this point you have one Hero in the field of battle and your opponent has one Evil Character in the field of battle, then you will either be in a losing, mutual destruction, stalemate, or winning situation.

   a) If you are currently losing the battle, you may play one or more good enhancement cards with your Hero until you are no longer losing or until you decide not to play another card.

   Note: When the total offensive strength of the Hero in the field of battle is greater than or equal to the total defensive toughness of the blocking Evil Character, then the Evil Character is considered to be losing the battle. When the total offensive strength of the Evil Character which is blocking is greater than or equal to the total defensive toughness of the Hero, then the Hero is considered to be losing the battle.

   *Example: **Daniel**, a Hero having an ability of 6/7, has an offensive strength of six and a defensive toughness of seven. In other words, when this Hero strikes an Evil Character he does six points of damage and is defeated when he receives seven or more points of damage. Thus a 6/6 Evil Character which is blocking would be losing the battle to **Daniel**, a 6/7 Hero. On the other hand, **Daniel**, a 6/7 Hero, would be considered to be losing a battle with a blocking 8/7 Evil Character such as **Witch of Endor**.*

   b) If you are in a stalemate situation where neither character is winning or losing the battle, then the player who did not play the last card may play the next enhancement card or pass the initiative which would allow the opponent the choice to play the next enhancement card or pass the initiative back.

c) If the rescuing and blocking characters are in a mutual destruction situation (when both would be discarded), then the player who did not play the last card may play the next enhancement card or pass allowing the opponent the choice of playing the next enhancement card or passing the initiative back.

d) If your Hero is winning the battle at this point, then your opponent may play one or more evil enhancement cards with the blocking Evil Character until no longer losing or until deciding not to play another card.

Note: The rescuer may only play good enhancement cards (cards with a Bible icon) on the Hero that is in the field of battle. The opponent may only play evil enhancement cards (cards with a skull icon) on the blocking Evil Character in the field of battle.

5) The player who is losing after an enhancement card is played plays the next enhancement card. Enhancement cards are then played until one player either can't or won't continue to battle.

6) Total the damage inflicted during the battle.

7) There are several possible results when resolving the Battle Phase.

a) If the Evil Character does enough damage to defeat the Hero, then the rescue attempt is unsuccessful and the Hero is discarded. (A healing card may be played at this point to keep a Hero from being discarded.)

b) If neither character defeats the other because of a stalemate situation, then the rescue attempt is unsuccessful, the Lost Soul remains in the Land of Bondage, both characters are returned to their own territories and all enhancement cards are discarded.

c) If the Hero and the Evil Character defeat each other (mutual destruction), then both are discarded, but the rescue attempt is successful and a Lost Soul, if available, must be surrendered to the rescuer. A Hero is willing to give his or her own life to rescue a Lost Soul.

d) If your rescuing Hero has dealt enough damage to the blocking Evil Character to defeat it, the Evil Character is discarded and your opponent chooses a Lost Soul, if one is available, to surrender to you. When a Lost Soul card is rescued, it is no longer defined or treated as a Lost Soul, it is now a Redeemed Soul and is placed in your Land of Redemption.

8) Regardless of the results of the battle, all non-character cards currently in the field of battle must be discarded, the surviving characters returned to their owner's territory, and the defeated characters discarded.

Discard Phase

After you have completed all the actions you choose in this turn and have resolved the Battle Phase (if necessary) you must not end your turn with more than eight cards in your hand. If you have eight or fewer cards in your hand, then announce that you are finished and the next player will begin a turn. If you have more than eight cards in your hand, then you must reduce the number of cards in your hand to no more than eight by one or more of the following actions:

a) Placing character cards into your territory.

b) Initiating a set-aside period by playing a set-aside card with a character card of the appropriate color brigade.

c) Discarding cards onto the top of your discard pile.

WINNING THE GAME

Play continues until one player has rescued five Lost Souls and placed them in his or her own Land of Redemption to win the game.

THE CARDS OF *REDEMPTION*™

This section identifies the cards in the game, gives general ideas of how some cards are played, and explores the strengths and weaknesses of the brigades.

There are several kinds of cards in the *Redemption*™ game. There are good characters which are called Heroes. The bad characters are referred to as Evil Characters. The good enhancement cards are played on Heroes. The evil enhancement cards are played on Evil Characters. The character and enhancement cards are divided into brigades of different colors. The Specialty cards tend to be the most powerful in the game, because they can be played at any time and their effects happen the instant they are played. The power enhancement cards are not limited to one brigade and can be played on any of the characters in the appropriate good or evil forces. The Lost Soul cards are rescued as players try to win the game.

There are 274 differently named cards in the game. This includes two different **Bow and Arrow** cards and two different **Angel Food** cards which are in different brigades and count as different cards for deck building. Some cards have different variations of text or art work printed on the card; but you may not count variants as being different cards for deck building purposes.

You will notice that some cards have special instructions printed on the front of the card. These special ability cards tend to be the stronger enhancement cards and add a great deal of excitement to the game. Rules and helpful hints for playing the special ability cards are explained in the **CARDS WITH SPECIAL ABILITIES** section.

COLOR BRIGADES

The character cards in *Redemption*™ are divided into color brigades. There are between six and ten characters in each of the twelve brigades. You will find 47 different Heroes and 44 different Evil Characters for a total of 91 character cards in the game.

Each color brigade has several enhancement cards of the same color which may be played with the character cards to increase their offensive or defensive values or affect cards or the game play in some way. There are currently 100 different color brigade enhancement cards for the Heroes and 61 different color brigade enhancement cards for the Evil Characters for a total of 161 color specific enhancement cards in the game.

The Heroes are divided into six color brigades that are designated by the color of the icon box in the top left corner of the card. The colors of the brigades in the Army of God are :

Blue

Gold

Green

Purple

Red

White

The Evil Characters are divided into six color brigades that are designated by the color of the icon box in the top left corner of the card. The colors of the Evil Forces brigades are :

Black

Brown

Crimson

Gold

Gray

Pale Green

This section examines the cards in each of the color brigades, explores some of the strengths and weaknesses of the brigades, and suggests strategy hints to keep in mind when building and playing your own customized decks.

Blue Brigade

"And thou shalt make the robe of the ephod all of blue." — *Exodus 28:31*

Blue is descriptive of heavenly character. The ephod is an official garment (like a fine decorative vest) worn by priests in the days of Moses.

The eight Heroes in the Blue Brigade are:
Jonah (7/5)
Anna (5/5)
Zephaniah (5/4)
Rebekah (4/4)
Mark (4/4)
Hannah (4/4)
Barnabas (4/4)
Silas (4/4)

The 17 enhancement cards in the Blue Brigade are:

Chastisement of the Lord (Set Hero aside for three turns. On turn four Hero returns with abilities increased 6/6.)

Stillness (Hero may withdraw from battle unharmed. All enhancement cards played may be returned to the player's hand except this one.)

Balm of Gilead (Heal any Hero from the Blue Brigade that is being discarded.)

Cup of Wrath (Holder may take any two Evil Characters in play and cause them to fight each other. The loser is discarded.)

Iron Pan (Set Hero aside. Hero gains 1/1 for each turn Hero mourns.)

Obedience of Noah (1/1, Holder may choose the Evil Character that his opponent uses to block his rescue attempt.) [**Obedience of Noah** (3/3, promotional card found in SCRYE™ magazine, #8)]

Patience of Job (1/1, Hero ignores Black Brigade.)

Strength (3/3)

Drawn Sword (3/2)

Measuring Line (3/2)

Courage (2/2)

Faith (2/2)

Faith of Abraham (2/2)

Love (2/2)

Truthfulness of Nathan (2/2)

Razor (2/1)

Rod of Iron (2/1)

Note: There is a limited edition variant of the **Balm of Gilead** card which states *"Heal any Hero from the Blue Brigade that is about to be discarded."* Play **Balm of Gilead** in all cases as though it has *"that is being discarded"* printed on it.

One advantage when playing Blue Brigade is that all of the Heroes have a low enough defensive toughness so that when battling the average 6/6 Evil Character, your Hero would play the first enhancement card after initially meeting in the field of battle.

There are no Blue Brigade enhancement cards which will guarantee a successful rescue attempt. The strongest enhancement cards are **Obedience of Noah** and **Cup of Wrath**. Clever use of these cards may win you that Lost Soul, but you cannot always use these cards effectively. Since many players will have the Black Brigade in their decks, because of the two 10/10 characters, ignoring Black Brigade with **Patience of Job** can come in handy. The special ability cards also include two set-aside cards, and a blue healing card. Blue Brigade is strong in the numbers category with **Obedience of Noah** (the promotional card) and **Strength** both being 3/3 cards as well as the two 3/2 cards and five 2/2 cards. But the reality is that the special ability cards win most of the rescue attempts if you are playing with people who have customized their decks.

The Blue Brigade would probably need to be one of three brigades in your deck, because it does not have enough sure winners to stand as the only Army of God brigade.

Gold Brigade

"And the building of the wall of it was of jasper: and the city was pure gold, like unto clear glass." — Revelation 21:18

Pure, clear gold is the precious material of which the city of new Jerusalem is to be built.

In the limited edition print run, the color in the icon box is yellow. In later print runs the color has been adjusted so it has more of a gold tint. All Army of God cards with either the yellow or the gold colors in the icon box are Gold Brigade cards and are played together.

The eight Heroes in the Gold Brigade are:
Moses (8/6)
Simeon (7/6)
Huldah (7/5)
Gideon (6/6)
Samson (6/6)
Samuel (4/4)
Deborah (4/4)
Othniel (4/4)

The 15 enhancement cards in the Gold Brigade are:

Furnace of God's Wrath (Holder may select one Evil Character in the Field of Play from each opponent and discard it.)

Plague of Flies (All Evil Characters in play decrease 6/6 for remainder of turn. If result is */0 or less; discard character(s).)

Prayer and Fasting (Set Hero aside. Hero gains 1/1 for every turn Hero prays. Discard after Hero returns.)

Two Olive Branches (A second Hero from the Gold Brigade may be added to the battle for one turn.)

Highway (Hero may withdraw from battle unharmed. All enhancement cards played may be returned to the player's hand except this one.)

Kindness (1/1, Hero ignores Red/Crimson Brigade.)

Peace (1/1, Hero ignores Black Brigade.)

Brass Serpent (Renders all poisons harmless.)

Angel Food (3/3, Essen 95 promotional card)

Hammer of God (4/2)

Dedication of Samuel (2/2)

Faithfulness of Luke (2/2)

Fearlessness of Joshua (2/2)

Humility of Moses (2/2)

Wisdom (2/2)

Note: Due to an oversight, some of the unlimited edition versions of the **Kindness** cards have a cross icon instead of a Bible icon, **Kindness** is not a Hero. All **Kindness** cards should be played as Gold Brigade enhancement cards.

The Gold Brigade has four characters with a defensive toughness of six which allows them to stand up to the average 6/6 Evil Character. Gold Brigade also has four characters with a toughness of four which would allow a player to play the first enhancement card during a rescue attempt, because initially there would be at best a mutual destruction situation against any Evil Character.

When looking at the enhancement card possibilities we find a winner in **Furnace of God's Wrath** allowing you to discard the blocking Evil Character (as well as an Evil Character from each of the other players in a multi-player game). There are two ignore cards and a banding card which give you a good chance of winning another Lost Soul or two with this brigade. There is a set-aside card which allows you to strengthen the abilities of a Hero and even to save a Hero which is losing in battle and about to be discarded. **Highway** can save a Hero (and any enhancement cards already played) that is losing a battle. **Hammer of God** (4/2) and **Angel Food** (3/3 promotional card given out at Essen '95 game fair in Germany) add good bonuses along with the five 2/2 cards. If you are playing the advanced rule which doubles the abilities of an enhancement card when played on a character of the same name, then **Humility of Moses** and **Dedication of Samuel** become 4/4 when played with their respective Heroes. Although the Gold Brigade will probably not be strong enough by itself, it would be a good choice as one of the color brigades in your deck.

Green Brigade

"But I am like a green olive tree in the house of God: I trust in the mercy of God for ever and ever." — Psalm 52:8

Green is a color often used in the Bible when describing the growth and life of the best places in the promised land. Green is descriptive of spiritual life and also symbolic of eternal life through Christ Jesus.

The eight Heroes of the Green Brigade are:
The Watchman (8/4)
Isaiah (7/8)
Amos (6/3)
Zechariah (5/6)
Agabus (5/4)
Miriam (4/4)
Cornelius (4/4)
Faithful Servant (4/4)

The 15 enhancement cards of the Green Brigade are:

Valley of Dry Bones (Return all Heroes from all discard piles to the Field of Play.)

Aaron's Rod (All Evil Enchantment cards now in play must be discarded.)

Repentance (Place this card on any human Evil Character in play and convert to a Green Brigade Hero.)

Bread of Life (Heal a Hero from the Green Brigade that is about to be discarded and increase 2/2 until Hero is discarded.)

Stone Cut without Hands (3/1, Holder ignores The Great Image card.)

Clemency of David (1/1, Hero ignores Brown Brigade.)

Live Coal (4/2)

Golden Lamp Stand (3/2)

Commitment of Paul (2/2)

Determination of Nehemiah (2/2)

Endurance (2/2)

Forcefulness of Isaiah (2/2)

Patience (2/2)

Banner of Love (2/1)

Ointment (0/2)

Note: Some limited edition **Bread of Life** cards do not state *"until Hero is discarded"*. Play this card as though *"until Hero is discarded"* is printed on it.

The Green Brigade hosts the Hero with the highest defense in **Isaiah** (7/8) and one of the two Heroes with the highest offensive strength in **The Watchman** (8/4). There are also five Heroes with a defensive toughness of four or less. So Green Brigade has a couple of strong offensive characters when you need to go for the large numbers in a rescue attempt as well as several characters which will be able to play the first enhancement card during a Battle Phase.

The Green Brigade has the only card that can bring back your Heroes from the discard pile, but it also does the same for all the other players in the game. There is a card to discard the evil enhancement cards that have been played, one that ignores Brown Brigade, and one which allows you to ignore the **Great Image** card. There is a card that will change a human Evil Character into a Green Brigade Hero, and you may play this on one of your own characters or use it to stop an Evil Character from blocking a rescue attempt. There is a healing card which strengthens a Green Brigade Hero by 2/2. The **Forcefulness of Isaiah** becomes a 4/4 when played on **Isaiah** if you are playing with the name-on-name advanced rule. There is a 4/2 and a 3/2 along with four 2/2 enhancement cards when your Hero has to battle by the numbers. Green Brigade has some of the most interesting enhancement cards in the game, but still is best suited to be played with another color or two.

Purple Brigade

"And the weight of the golden earrings that he requested was a thousand and seven hundred shekels of gold; beside ornaments, and collars, and purple raiment that was on the kings of Midian, and beside the chains that were about their camels' necks."
— Judges 8:26

Purple is a color associated with royalty in Biblical times.

The seven Heroes of the Purple Brigade are:
Elisha (7/5)
Ezekiel (7/4)
Esther (6/6)
Jonathan (6/6)
Habakkuk (6/3)
John (5/5)
Hosea (5/4)

The 17 enhancement cards of the Purple Brigade are:

Authority of Christ (All Evil Characters in play must be discarded.)

Ezekiel's Stick (A second Hero may join the battle this turn.)

River Flowing from Temple (Add a Hero from your hand to the battle.)

The Vineyard (Holder may take all Purple Brigade Heroes in his Territory and set them aside for two turns to increase them by 4/4.)

Meditation (Set Hero aside. Hero gains 1/1 for every turn Hero meditates. Discard after Hero returns.)

The Branch (A male Hero's abilities increase by fifty percent of the value printed on the Hero card.)

Elisha's Bones (Heal any Hero that is being discarded and increase abilities 2/2.)

Leaves for Healing (Heal a Hero from the Purple Brigade that is about to be discarded.)

Speed (3/2, Hero gains first-strike ability.)

Hinds' Feet (3/1)

Alertness (2/2)

Courage of Esther (2/2)

Gentleness (2/2)

Joy (2/2)

Long-suffering of John (2/2)

Loyalty of Jonathan (2/2)

Mercy of James (2/2)

Note: Some limited edition **Ezekiel's Stick** cards read: "*Holder may add a second Hero to the battle for one turn.*" Play these cards as though they were the same.

The Purple Brigade has two Heroes with a seven offensive strength and three with a six offensive strength. Three of the Heroes have a defensive toughness of four or three. That means there is a good balance of Heroes who will start off well when trying to build offensive points and others who will always be allowed to play the first special ability enhancement card when making a rescue attempt.

The Purple Brigade has nine enhancement cards with special abilities plus eight other enhancement cards. Playing **Authority of Christ** will probably win you a Lost Soul by causing a blocking Evil Character to be discarded. It takes all of the Evil Characters out of the game so be sure to play it when you have saved a couple in your hand for defending Lost Souls in your own Land of Bondage. There are two banding cards, two healing cards, and two set-aside cards in the Purple Brigade. There is also a first-strike card and a card which increases the abilities of a male Hero.

Three of the Heroes also have 2/2 enhancement cards with their names on them which would add 4/4 when played on their respective Heroes, if you are playing by the name-on-name advanced rule.

Purple Brigade is a strong color brigade which might be able to stand by itself in your deck as the only brigade, but adding another color will add more sure winner enhancement cards to your deck and increase your chances of easily winning more rescue attempts.

Red Brigade

"The shield of his mighty men is made red, the valiant men are in scarlet: the chariots shall be with flaming torches in the day of his preparation, and the fir trees shall be terribly shaken." — Nahum 2:3

Red is descriptive of military might and most of the Heroes in this brigade are warriors.

The ten Heroes in the Red Brigade are:
Malachi (7/5)
Adino (6/6)
Joab (6/6)
Shamgar (6/6)
Uriah (6/6)
Gad (6/3)
Asahel (4/4)
Christian Soldier (4/4)
Hushai (4/4)
Mighty Warrior (4/4) [**Mighty Warrior** (6/6), promo card for *Heroes Convention*, Charlotte]

The 21 enhancement cards in the Red Brigade are:

Wheel within a Wheel (Holder may exchange current Hero with any Hero from holder's draw pile. Shuffle after exchange.)

Baggage (Take any Evil Character prisoner and place in your Land of Bondage. Character is treated as a Lost Soul.)

Sound the Alarm (Holder may add a second Hero to the fight for one turn.)

Potter and the Clay (Set Hero aside. Hero gains 1/1 for every turn Hero is set aside.)

David's Sling (3/1, Hero gains first-strike ability.)

Forest Fire (2/2, Hero ignores Pale Green Brigade.)

Healing (Heal any Hero that is about to be discarded.)

Arrow of Deliverance (4/2)

Bravery of David (2/2)

David's Staff (2/2)

Goodness (2/2)

Hope (2/2)

Steadfastness of Peter (2/2)

Temperance (2/2)

Bow and Arrow (2/1)

Battle Axe (2/0)

Ehud's Dagger (2/0)

Five Smooth Stones (2/0)

Buckler (0/2)

Coat of Mail (0/2)

Helmet of Brass (0/2)

The Red Brigade has seven Heroes (when counting the promo card) with an offensive strength of six or higher—that is more than any other Army of God color brigade. Five of the Heroes have a defensive toughness of four or less which enables them to play the first enhancement card during a rescue attempt.

Baggage will take a blocking Evil Character out of the field of battle, but it is then available as a Lost Soul for an opponent to rescue. There is a banding card, a set-aside card, a healing card, and an ignore pale Green Brigade card. If you are playing a 4/4 Hero and are losing a battle by a point or two, playing Wheel within a Wheel will allow you to trade for a stronger Hero. The 4/2 and 3/1 first strike cards come in handy. There are six 2/2 enhancement cards and seven other cards with lesser abilities.

Red Brigade might be able to stand by itself, but works better in a two color brigade Army of God deck to give Sound the Alarm and Wheel within a Wheel their best chance of winning a Lost Soul.

White Brigade

"And I saw a great white throne, and him that sat on it, from whose face the earth and the heaven fled away; and there was found no place for them." — Revelation 20:11

White is descriptive of glory and majesty. It represents a pure and sinless nature and is often associated with saints, angels, or an encounter with a brilliant light indicating the presence of God.

The six Hero cards of the White Brigade are:
Jeremiah (7/7)
John the Baptist (7/4)
Daniel (6/7)
Mary (6/6) [**Mary** (promo) 6/6, increases 3/3 in December]
Philip's Daughters (5/4)
Ruth (4/4)

The 15 enhancement cards in the White Brigade are:

Lion Dwelling with the Calf (2/2, Blocking Evil Character refuses to block. Opponent must present a new blocker or rescue is successful.)

Charred Vine (Set Hero aside for five turns. On turn six Hero returns with abilities increased 7/7.)

Sleep (Set Hero aside. Hero gains 1/1 for every turn Hero sleeps. Discard after Hero awakes.)

Wall of Fire (2/2, Black Brigade and Pale Green Brigade characters have no effect on current rescue attempt.)

Compassion of Jeremiah (1/1, Hero ignores Red/Crimson Brigade)

Devotion of Ruth (1/1, Hero ignores Gray Brigade.)

Meekness of Isaac (1/1, Hero ignores Gold Brigade.)

Submissiveness of Mary (1/1, Hero ignores Pale Green Brigade.)

Antidote (1/1, Renders all poisons harmless.)

Mountain of God (4/2)

Angel Food (3/3)

Floating Ax Head (3/2)

Banner (2/2)

Forgiveness of Joseph (2/2)

Purity of Enoch (2/2)

There are four Heroes with an offensive strength of six or greater and three with a defensive toughness of four or less. So the Heroes are balanced for going for the offensive victory or playing for the first enhancement card. The promotional card of **Mary** receives an increase of 3/3 in abilities during the month of December which makes her the strongest Hero in the game at 9/9.

The enhancement cards are strong when it comes to ignoring the evil colors because the White Brigade only lacks an *"ignore the Brown Brigade"* card. There are two set-aside cards and a card which makes your opponent choose another blocker. Three of the enhancement cards have character names which match in this color if you are playing by name-on-name advanced rule to increase the strength of those Heroes. There are enhancement cards with abilities of 4/2, 3/3, and 3/2 as well as three others of 2/2.

White Brigade could stand by itself, but is best played with another color that has some winners or some banding cards, to pull a White Brigade Hero into a battle at the right time to use one of the many ignore cards.

Black Brigade

"Raging waves of the sea, foaming out their own shame; wandering stars, to whom is reserved the blackness of darkness for ever." — Jude 13

In the Bible, the color black is often descriptive of darkness and fear of the unknown. It is analogous with a sinful and evil heart. The darkness represents calamity and separation from God in the eternal void and loneliness of Hell.

The seven Evil Characters in the Black Brigade are:
Abaddon the Destroyer (10/10)
Goliath (10/10)
Damsel with Spirit of Divination (6/7)
Prophets of Samaria (6/7)
Locust from the Pit (6/6)
Manasseh (6/6)
Shemaiah (4/4)

The ten Black Brigade enhancement cards are:

Hunger (All Heroes of one opponent decrease 6/6 for remainder of turn. If result is */0 or less, discard Hero.)

Net (2/2, Take any Hero prisoner and place Hero in your Land of Bondage. Hero is treated as a Lost Soul.)

Yoke of Iron (Opponent must select and discard two of his enhancements currently in the Field of Battle.)

Woman in the Ephah (2/3, This card is worth 3/4 if played against Red Brigade.)

Vain Vision (2/2, 4/4 if played against a prophet.)

Manasseh's Altar (2/2, Evil Character repels White Brigade.)

Hate (Evil Character repels Green Brigade.)

Goat with Horn (2/3)

Goliath's Spear (2/1)

Poison (2/0)

This color has two strong 10/10 characters, as well as two 6/7, two 6/6 and a 4/4 character. There are six different enhancement cards which can be played with the tough characters to make them hard to beat by the numbers. The 4/4 character can be strategically played against a more powerful Hero to ensure playing an enhancement card first.

The enhancement cards include a block with **Net**, but this puts a character in your Land of Bondage for a player to rescue. There are two cards which repel specific colors. **Hunger** will help reduce the good forces of one opponent and might be just enough for a block, plus it is very effective against a banded attack. **Yoke of Iron** makes your opponent discard two enhancements and there are a couple of other cards that receive extra bonuses in certain situations.

The Black Brigade can be played as the only defensive color brigade for the evil forces, but it is best played with another color brigade such as the Gold, Gray, or Brown Brigade.

Brown Brigade

"And the fourth angel poured out his vial upon the sun; and power was given unto him to scorch men with fire. And men were scorched with great heat, and blasphemed the name of God, which hath power over these plagues: and they repented not to give him glory." — *Revelation 16:8-9*

Brown is descriptive of being scorched and rebellious (from the Hebrew word *Chuwm*; "to be warm", i.e. by implication here, "to be sunburnt").

The seven Evil Characters in the Brown Brigade are:
Beast from the Earth (10/10)
Enchanter (6/7)
Delilah (6/6, Samson and his strength have no effect on Delilah.)
Ahab (6/6)
Haman (6/6)
Shimei (6/6)
Ahaziah (5/7)

The ten Brown Brigade enhancement cards are:

Dungeon of Malchiah (Take any Hero prisoner and place Hero in your opponent's Land of Bondage. Hero is treated as a Lost Soul.)

Ignorance (All Heroes in play decrease 4/4 for remainder of turn. If result is */0 or less, discard Hero.)

Cage (Return any Hero to owner's hand.)

Paul's Girdle (Return any Hero to owner's hand.)

Molten Calf Worship (Set Evil Character aside for 5 turns. Character returns with abilities increased 4/8.)

Cruelty (1/1, Evil Character repels White Brigade.)

Bad Figs (2/3, Note: this card is considered a poison.)

Boils (2/2)

Axe (2/1)

Image of Jealousy (1/3)

The Brown Brigade has one of the 10/10 Evil Characters. Five have a six strength and one has a five strength. Defensively, two are at seven and four are at six. In a battle Brown Brigade Evil Characters would only have the initiative to play an enhancement card first when the rescuer plays one of the Heroes with a defensive toughness greater than five.

The enhancement cards are very powerful for a single brigade. There are three definite stoppers with **Paul's Girdle**, **Cage**, and **Dungeon of Malchiah**. **Cruelty** repels the White Brigade. **Ignorance** will eliminate the Heroes in your opponent's territory that will position him to play the first enhancement card on his next turn. Imagine setting **Beast from the Earth** aside with **Molten Calf Worship** near the beginning of the game and bringing it back in as 14/18! **Bad Figs** can be countered by an anti-poison card.

The Brown Brigade is strong enough to stand alone as a single defensive color. Playing Brown Brigade with another color brigade such as the Black, Gray, or Pale Green Brigade would provide an extremely strong defensive deck.

Crimson Brigade

"And there appeared another wonder in heaven; and behold a great red dragon, having seven heads and ten horns, and seven crowns upon his heads." —*Revelation 12:3*

"Come now, and let us reason together, saith the LORD: though your sins be as scarlet, they shall be as white as snow; though they be red like crimson, they shall be as wool." —*Isaiah 1:18*

Crimson is descriptive of persecution and sin.

Crimson was originally printed in the limited edition as red in the icon box. There is no evil Red Brigade. All evil enhancement cards and characters with the color red in the icon box should be considered to be in the Crimson Brigade and played accordingly. In the limited edition, **Kindness** and **Compassion of Jeremiah** allow the Hero to ignore Red Brigade, but this should be understood to mean *"Hero ignores Crimson Brigade."* Cards printed after the limited edition have corrected colors and text. Although the color in the icon boxes match in the limited edition, the Red Brigade Army of God cards and the evil forces Crimson Brigade cards may not be played together.

The nine Evil Characters in the Crimson Brigade are:
Red Dragon (10/10)
Whore of Babylon (8/8)
Nebuchadnezzar (6/8)
Prophets of Baal (6/7)
Jezebel (6/6)
Judas Iscariot (6/6)
Salome (6/6)
Stone Throwers (6/6)
Belshazzar (5/6)

The 11 Crimson Brigade enhancement cards are:

Great Image (All opponents' Heroes in play that are not in the Field of Battle at the end of this battle must be discarded.)

Covenant with Death (Set Evil Character aside. Character gains 1/1 for every turn Character is set aside.)

Four Horns (No good banding cards can be played this turn. Any currently in play are discarded.)

Vain Philosophy (1/1, Evil Character repels Purple Brigade.)

Baal Worship (Evil Character may not repent this turn.)

Weeping for Tammuz (2/3)

Chariots of Iron (2/2)

Discord (2/2)

Fiery Darts (2/2)

Treachery (2/2)

First Figs (1/4)

The Crimson Brigade has one 10/10 character and one 8/8 character, giving this color two strong offensive cards. Most of the other cards have an average offensive strength of six. Four characters have a defensive ability above six; none are lower than six. This gives the color a good chance to win by the numbers. There is little chance of getting to play the first enhancement card when characters meet in battle. The Crimson Brigade actually has four characters tough enough to defeat a 6/6 Hero when alone in battle.

The **Great Image** card has a good chance of blocking a rescue attempt. **Four Horns** prevents Heroes from banding, and that is a nice limitation to place on an opponent attempting to put another color Hero into the field of battle to ignore or defeat a Crimson Brigade blocker. The Crimson Brigade has a repel Purple Brigade card and even a set-aside card. **Baal Worship** must be played before **Repentance**, so play it in anticipation of protecting a blocking human Evil Character when facing the Green Brigade. The 2/3 and 1/4 enhancement cards are especially helpful to build up the defensive capabilities of a character. There are also four 2/2 enhancement cards.

The Crimson Brigade is especially strong against the Purple Brigade because of the repel and anti-banding cards; however, it is probably not quite strong enough to stand alone as the only defensive brigade from the evil forces.

Gold Brigade

"Thou hast also taken thy fair jewels of my gold and of my silver, which I had given thee, and madest to thyself images of men, and didst commit whoredom with them," —Ezekiel 16:17

Gold is the valuable and coveted metal commonly used in making graven images for idol worshipers.

In the limited edition the Gold Brigade cards have a yellowish-greenish color in the icon box. The color is more of a golden color for the unlimited and Prophets cards. Although the color in the icon box may be a different shade, all these cards are used together as the Gold Brigade.

The six Evil Characters in the Gold Brigade are:
Users of Curious Arts (6/7)
Herodias (6/6)
Jaazaniah (6/6)
Pharaoh (6/6)
Task Master (6/6)
Astrologers (5/8)

The nine enhancement cards of the Gold Brigade are:

Lies (Owner may choose the Hero his opponent uses to rescue.)

Den of Robbers (A second Evil Character from the Gold Brigade may join the battle.)

Ram with Two Horns (A second Evil Character from Black Brigade may join the battle.)

Abandonment (1/1, Evil Character repels Red Brigade.)

The Flying Scroll (3/3)

The Girdle (2/4)

Grief (2/2)

Stone of Thebez (2/2)

Paintings of Abominations (1/4)

The Gold Brigade characters are all basically average. The enhancement cards which increase a character's abilities are good. There are two banding cards and one card which allows you to choose a different Hero for the battle. There is one enhancement card which repels Red Brigade Heroes.

Gold Brigade is not strong enough to be the only defensive brigade in your deck. This color brigade pairs well with the Black Brigade because of the banding card **Ram with Two Horns**. Gold Brigade will work best as one of two-or-three defensive colors in your deck.

Gray Brigade

"I know thy works, that thou art neither cold nor hot: I would thou wert cold or hot. So then because thou art lukewarm, and neither cold nor hot, I will spew thee out of my mouth." —Revelation 3:15-16

We often speak of the gray areas in life as being those issues which are difficult to know right from wrong. We see black and white fade to shades of gray. Gray describes people who are neither hot nor cold.

The eight Evil Characters of the Gray Brigade are:
The False Prophet (8/12)
Balaam (6/7)
Abihu (6/6)
False Shepherds (6/6)
False Teachers (6/6)
Hard-hearted Religious Leaders (6/6)
Chaldeans (5/7)
False Prophets (4/4)

The nine enhancement cards in the Gray Brigade are:

False Peace (Holder may look through his draw pile and select one card and continue fighting. Shuffle draw pile after play.)

Snare (Take any Hero prisoner and place Hero in your Land of Bondage. Hero is treated as a Lost Soul.)

Chains (Return any Hero to owner's hand.)

Molech Worship (Set Evil Character aside. Character gains 1/1 for every turn character worships Molech.)

False Wisdom (Holder may look at rescuer's hand.)

False Dreams (Next player may not make a rescue attempt his next turn.)

Wildness (1/1, Evil Character repels Gold Brigade.)

False Prophesy (Evil Character repels any non-prophet.)

Bow and Arrow (2/1)

The Gray Brigade has the powerful 8/12 **The False Prophet** card and the 4/4 **False Prophets** card. The six other characters have average abilities. **The False Prophet** is difficult to beat by the numbers and **False Prophets** has a low strength and toughness to allow you to sometimes play the first enhancement card when characters meet in the field of battle.

The enhancement cards are powerful and twist the normal game play in clever and unexpected ways. **Chains** and **Snare** immediately stop a battle. **False Peace** allows you to bring into play just the right card for the situation. There is a repel Gold Brigade and a powerful repel any non-prophet card which works against many of the Heroes. **False Dreams** is mainly used in a multi-player game, but there is a way to use it in a two-player game without causing yourself to lose a turn. Can you figure out that combo? The set-aside card might best be used to save a character who is losing in battle from being discarded. **Bow and Arrow** is one of only two cards in the game to have another card in a different brigade with the same name. Only the White Brigade has an ignore Gray Brigade card. Not only does **False Peace** allow you to look through your deck, but **False Wisdom** allows you to take a look at the rescuing player's hand. What a sneaky brigade!

Gray Brigade can stand alone in a deck as the defensive brigade because of two sure stoppers, three probable stoppers and the possibility of taking two turns in a row. Using two brigades, however, will make your defense stronger and more adaptable to game situations.

Pale Green Brigade

"And I looked, and behold a pale horse: and his name that sat on him was Death, and Hell followed with him. And power was given unto them over the fourth part of the earth, to kill with sword, and with hunger, and with death, and with the beasts of the earth." —Revelation 6:8

Pale Green is descriptive of death. The King James version uses the word "pale". The actual word used by John here was the Greek word *Chloros*, or "greenish", from the Greek word *chloe* or "green".

In the limited edition the evil forces Pale Green Brigade bears the same shade of green as in the icon boxes of the Army of God Green Brigade cards. The color has been adjusted to a pale green shade on the unlimited and Prophets cards. All of the evil forces cards with either shade of green in their icon boxes should be played together as the Pale Green Brigade.

Although the colors in the icon box match, in the limited edition, the Green Brigade Army of God cards and the evil forces Pale Green Brigade cards may not be played together.

The seven Evil Character cards in the Pale Green Brigade are:
Beast from the Sea (10/10)
Witch of Endor (8/7)
Wizards (6/7)
Prince of Persia (6/6, **The Angel of the Lord** has no effect on this card unless **Daniel** is in the field of Battle.)
Doeg (6/6)
Frog Demons (6/6)
Workers with Familiar Spirits (4/4)

The 12 enhancement cards for Pale Green Brigade are:

Confusion (Owner may look through one opponent's draw pile, discard one card and shuffle remaining cards.)

Rage (Two Evil Characters of 6/6 or less may band together.)

Torn Mantle (No good banding cards can be played this turn. Any currently in play are discarded.)

Stocks (Take any Hero prisoner and place Hero in your Land of Bondage. Hero is treated as a Lost Soul.)

Filthy Garments (Selected Hero's abilities decrease 4/4 for remainder of turn.)

Large Tree (Set Evil Character aside. Character gains 1/1 for every turn it is set aside.)

Darkness (2/0, Evil Character repels Blue Brigade.)

Ashtaroth Worship (3/3) [There are two different illustrated versions of this card.]

Strange Vine (2/4)

Chariots of the Sun (2/2)

Evil (2/2)

Lance (2/2)

The Pale Green Brigade has one of the powerful 10/10 characters and one of the sneaky 4/4 characters. The 8/7 **Witch of Endor** is a strong character, but the other characters are of average strength and toughness.

The Pale Green Brigade has a good variety of enhancement cards. **Stocks** is a stopper. **Confusion** allows you to see what is in an opponent's draw pile and also discard a powerful card (such as the **Son of God** card to prevent an instant rescue). There are repel, banding, and prevent banding cards. Decreasing a Hero 4/4 can send a particularly bothersome foe to the discard pile. **Ashtaroth Worship** is printed with two different variations of the art work, but it is still the same name on the card in the same brigade, so you may only have a total of three of this card in your deck.

The Pale Green Brigade is best when used with another brigade for defense, because it is probably not quite strong enough to stand alone in most games.

POWER ENHANCEMENT CARDS

There are seven multi-colored power enhancement cards in the game. They are:

Sun Worship (3/3)

Shoes of Peace (3/3)

Sword of the Spirit (3/1)

Pillar of a Cloud (2/2, *Hero gainsFirst-Strike ability for this turn*)

Breastplate of Righteousness (0/4)

Shield of Faith (0/4)

Helmet of Salvation (0/4)

Sun Worship may be played upon an Evil Character of any color brigade.

The other six power enhancement cards are played with the Heroes of any color brigade. These power enhancement cards are often referred to by players as rainbow cards because of the rainbow-like coloring of the icon box. Since power enhancement cards are not limited to being played with a single matching color brigade like most enhancement cards, they are easy to play in situations when a battle will be decided by the numbers. The only disadvantage of these power enhancement cards is that many battles are won with special ability cards, and having all seven power cards in your deck lowers the probability of drawing a card of greater strategic usefulness.

SPECIALTY CARDS

There are four specialty cards. They are:

Son of God

Angel of the Lord

Christian Martyr

Burial

These cards affect the game the instant they are played. An opponent has no opportunity to counter a specialty card. Since they may be played at any time by any player in the game, these are the most strategically powerful cards in the game. You don't want to leave them out of your deck. These specialty cards are explained in detail in the **CARDS WITH SPECIAL ABILITIES** section.

LOST SOUL CARDS

Lost Soul cards are character cards that are held prisoner by the evil forces in a Land of Bondage. Once a Lost Soul character card is rescued, it is no longer defined as a Lost Soul because it is now a Redeemed Soul. There are ten Lost Soul cards and one **Lost Souls** card in the game. These cards are usually referred to by a brief description of the art or by the Scripture reference on the card. When a rescue attempt is successful the defending player chooses which Lost Soul to give to the rescuer.

Little Boy (Ezekiel 34:12)

Woman in Black (II Timothy 2:26)

Old Widow (I Kings 17:12)

Man with Dagger (II Timothy 3:6-7)

Seated Beggar (Luke 15:6)

Blind Man (Job 33:27-28)

Green Hand (Ephesians 5:14)

Lost Souls (Proverbs 22:14)

Man Knocking at Door (Luke 13:25)

Prisoner (Isaiah 42:7)

Beggar in White (Ezekiel 36:19)

Decks must contain a minimum of 50 cards including seven Lost Soul cards. For every seven cards beyond 50 one of those seven must be a Lost Soul. A deck of 56 cards contains only seven Lost Soul cards while a deck of 57 must contain eight Lost Soul cards. A deck of 57-63 cards contains eight Lost Soul cards while a deck of 64-70 cards contains nine Lost Soul cards. If you want to play a deck containing more cards, then you must add the appropriate numbers of Lost Soul cards.

Cards With Special Abilities

Many of the cards in *Redemption*™ have special abilities printed across the art-work. These cards affect game play or other cards in the game. Some of these special ability cards will have a delayed effect upon the game, while others will have effects which happen immediately after the card is played. In this section we will take a look at all of the special ability cards and give you some general information about the card type, the result of playing the card, and some strategy in using the card effectively.

INSTANT CARDS

You may play an Instant card at any time, even when you do not have a character in the field of battle, or when it is not your turn. A card which has a Lamb or Grim Reaper icon symbol in the top left corner is an instant card. You are limited to having only one of each of these powerful cards in your play deck.

Son of God

Result: Immediate rescue of a Lost Soul in play.

The single most powerful card in the *Redemption*™ game is the **Son of God** card which enables you to make an immediate rescue of any Lost Soul in play. This includes a Lost Soul being held captive in your own Land of Bondage, a common Land of Bondage, or even one of the two souls on the **Lost Souls** card. When there is only one Lost Soul card in your Land of Bondage you may play the **Son of God** card to rescue it in order to prevent it from being available for another player to rescue. This strategy is especially important when your opponent is about to make the fifth rescue. You may also want to save this card until you win your fourth rescue attempt and then play it to immediately win the game on that turn.

Angel of the Lord

Result: Immediate forced discard of an Evil Character in play.

The **Angel of the Lord** card may be played at any time to cause an Evil Character to be discarded. The best use of the **Angel of the Lord** card is to cause a blocking Evil Character to be discarded thus ensuring a successful rescue.

Burial

Result: Immediate forced discard of a Lost Soul in play.

When you play the **Burial** card, you may choose which Lost Soul in play is discarded. You may choose one of your own Lost Soul cards to be discarded to prevent an opponent from rescuing it. You may also cause an opponent to discard a Lost Soul card thus preventing it from being rescued by the **Son of God** card of that opponent or another opponent, but that would also mean one less Lost Soul in the game for you to rescue. The **Burial** card cannot be played in any player's Land of Redemption. Souls in the Land of Redemption are Redeemed Souls and by definition are no longer Lost Souls. **Burial** is useful to cancel out an opponent's rescue by playing it on the **Lost Souls** card after the first rescue to bury the remaining **Lost Soul** and to keep the first rescue from being counted.

Christian Martyr

Result: Immediate forced discard of any Hero in play.

When you play the **Christian Martyr** card, you may cause an opponent to discard a Hero that is about to make a successful rescue attempt. This stops the rescue unless there is already another banded Hero in the field of battle. In a multi-player game you may want to use **Christian Martyr** to stop an opponent from rescuing another opponent's Lost Soul card and to keep it available for your own rescue attempt.

DISCARD CARDS

Discard cards are enhancement cards which allow you to discard other character or enhancement cards. Some discard cards have an immediate effect and some have a delayed effect. Some affect only one card and others may affect many cards.

Authority of Christ

Result: All Evil Characters in play are immediately discarded.

The **Authority of Christ** card is one you may not want to play too early in the game. It has the greatest impact when your opponent has several Evil Characters in the field of play. When you play **Authority of Christ** your rescue is successful because it causes the blocking Evil Character to be discarded along with all of the Evil Characters in the game, including your own. Plan carefully for the right time to play this card. Hold one or more Evil Characters in your hand so you will still have defenders for the next turn.

Aaron's Rod

Result: All evil enhancement cards in play must be immediately discarded.

By playing **Aaron's Rod** when evil enhancements are in play, you will cause your opponent to waste valuable cards, and you'll increase your chances of making a successful rescue attempt. **Aaron's Rod** is especially useful in negating the special abilities of cards (by discarding them) which would have affected play at or until the end of the turn. This includes cards like: **Great Image**, **Torn Mantle**, **Four Horns**, **Baal Worship**, **Hunger**, **Filthy Garments**, or **Ignorance**. It cannot be played to negate the effects of enhancement cards such as: **Chains**, **Confusion**, **False Peace**, or **Net**, which have immediate effects. After **Aaron's Rod** is played, it is also discarded and cannot affect any further evil enhancement cards played during that turn.

Great Image

Result: All Heroes in play, except your own, which are not in the field of battle at the end of this battle must be discarded.

The **Great Image** card, when played after players have most of their Heroes in play, will significantly decrease all the other players' abilities to make successful rescue attempts for the next few turns.

You can stop the effects of **Great Image** from occurring by playing **Stone Cut without Hands** or **Aaron's Rod.** Playing **Angel of the Lord** or **Furnace of God's Wrath** would win the rescue attempt by discarding the Evil Character upon which **Great Image** has been activated, but since that action would also end the battle when the effects of **Great Image** occur, you would be sending many Heroes to the discard pile. If **Great Image** has been played with an Evil Character which has been banded, then discarding that character will nullify the special ability of **Great Image** because it will no longer be in the field of play when damage is dealt. If you are playing Green Brigade and you have held a character in your hand on your next turn, you may bring all Heroes in all discard piles back with **Valley of Dry Bones.** Another defense against **Great Image** is to use as many banding cards (**Sound the Alarm, Ezekiel's Stick, River Flowing from the Temple,** or **Two Olive Branches**) as you can because the more Heroes you can place into the field of battle the higher your offensive score will be and the more card play choices you will have. You may also use healing or set-aside cards to keep some of your Heroes from being discarded.

Furnace of God's Wrath

Result: Holder may immediately discard one Evil Character in the field of play from each opponent.

You may ensure a successful rescue by electing to discard the Evil Character blocking your rescue attempt. During a rescue attempt you may choose to play this card early in the battle phase to avoid any enhancements with immediate effects that your opponent may play against you, or you may take a risk and wait until later so your opponent will lose the character and expend some enhancement cards. If you wait until later in the battle, you may also be using up some of your own enhancements. In a multi-player game this card allows you to weaken the evil forces of all your opponents by discarding some strong Evil Characters.

Yoke of Iron

Result: Opponent must choose and immediately discard two good enhancements currently in the field of battle.

Like the **Furnace of God's Wrath**, this enhancement will take effect immediately when played. When forced to discard two of the enhancement cards already played, this card may severely weaken the chances of a Hero making a successful rescue attempt. This card may also be played when your opponent has only played one enhancement card, but since its effects are immediate and then it is also discarded, it will not affect any future enhancement cards your opponent may play. The **Yoke of Iron** may force your opponent to discard a banding card, but will not remove a second Hero from the field of battle if already played.

HEALING CARDS

Healing cards allow you to save a character card which is about to be discarded and return it to your territory. The ability of a healing card is activated by playing it on a character card in the field of battle. Some healing cards allow you to save any character and others only work with a specific color brigade. A healing card cannot save a character which is instantly or immediately discarded from the field of play because the character card is no longer in play for the healing card to be played on it (**Elisha's Bones** and **Balm of Gilead** are exceptions to this rule). If used when damage is dealt and before a character card is actually sent to the discard pile, a healing card may be extremely useful to save the only Hero of a color brigade left in your territory or hand. Healing a Hero which has had strength and toughness increased from being set aside allows that character to retain this extra strength.

General Healing Cards

Healing

Result: Heal any Hero that is about to be discarded.

This healing card enables you to return to your territory any Hero that has been defeated and is about to be discarded. A Hero which is healed may not return to the field of battle during the same turn. Healing cards are especially helpful when saving the only character left in a color brigade that you really can't afford to discard. When cards like **Ignorance** or **Hunger** threaten several characters in play, a healing card can save at least one.

Balm of Gilead
Elisha's Bones

Result: Heal any Hero that is being discarded.

Elisha's Bones has an extra ability which gives the healed character a permanent increase of 2/2 to strength and toughness for the remainder of the game or until that character card is discarded (actually placed on the top of the discard pile). Because of the unique wording of **Elisha's Bones** and **Balm of Gilead** healing cards, they may also be used to save a card which is being discarded by an instant card. These cards can be played with a Hero of matching brigade color in the field of battle or a Hero of matching brigade color that is being discarded.

Brigade Specific Healing Cards

These cards are used in the same way as general healing cards except they are limited to healing only the characters of a particular color brigade. **Bread of Life** also gives the Hero a permanent 2/2 increases in strength and toughness for the remainder of the game or until that character card is discarded.

Result: Heal any Hero of the stated color brigade that is about to be discarded.

Bread of Life

Heals Green Brigade Hero and increases abilities 2/2 for remainder of game or until character is discarded.

Leaves for Healing

Heals Purple Brigade Hero.

RETURN CARDS

Any card which returns another card to its previous position could be considered a return card. In a sense a healing card which returns a character to your territory could be considered a return card, but for game play you should only consider the following cards to be return cards.

Valley of Dry Bones

Result: Returns all Heroes from all discard piles back to their owner's territories.

Heroes returned to play in this way are played at face value losing any increase in strength or toughness gained from a previous set-aside or healing card. The **Valley of Dry Bones** card is best used to return to your territory a Hero or Heroes from a brigade for which you have enhancement cards you want to play. In a multi-player game, this card will probably bring several Heroes from several brigades back into the game so plan carefully for the best time to use this card. This card certainly delivers a great deal of excitement to the game when it sends many Heroes into play at the same time. You might want to use this card in the turn before you play **Great Image** or **Hunger**, which might send some of your opponent's characters back to the discard pile while allowing you to keep the Heroes which have been returned to your territory.

Return to Hand Cards

Paul's Girdle
Cage
Chains

Result: Immediately return any Hero in the field of play to the owner's hand.

Use these cards to immediately terminate a rescue attempt, thus preventing one of your Lost Souls from being rescued. Heroes must be in the field of play in order to be returned to their owner's hand. You can't use this card type on a Hero in a set-aside area or discard pile. Captured Heroes imprisoned in the Land of Bondage are within the field of play, but are treated as Lost Souls, not as Heroes. Discard any enhancement cards which have been played on a Hero card that is returned to the owner's hand. A Hero which is returned to the hand retains any permanent increases in strength and toughness gained by healing cards or set-aside periods. If you are about to play a card like **Hunger** or **Great Image**, you may want to return to your hand a Hero you can't strategically afford to lose. But these cards are almost too valuable as stoppers to be used in any other way.

CONVERSION CARD

A conversion card changes a card so that it is treated as something else.

Repentance

Result: Convert a human Evil Character card in play into a Green Brigade Hero card and treat the card as a Hero for the remainder of the game.

After playing (activating) this card on a Green Brigade Hero card in the field of battle, this card may then be placed on an Evil Character card to convert it into a Green Brigade Hero with the same offensive strength and defensive toughness as when it was an Evil Character. If the abilities of the converted character have been increased, then those additions remain with the new Hero for the rest of the game or until discarded. The newly converted Hero remains under the control of the player who owns the card.

Repentance is the only conversion card currently in the game and is a valuable card to stop a block and make a rescue. Since your Hero has no opposition, and your opponent cannot send another Evil Character into battle without a banding card, you win the rescue attempt.

You may also play this card on one of your own Evil Characters to provide another Green Brigade Hero for your Army of God. **Goliath**, if converted, would become a formidable 10/10 Hero.

CAPTURE CARDS

The instant you play one of these cards, the character you choose is captured before your opponent has an opportunity to respond. Playing a capture card is a guaranteed winner or stopper when capturing the only opposing character in the field of battle. If your opponent already has an ignore or repel card in the field of battle that protects the character from a specific brigade or card type, then a capture card of that brigade or card type would be ineffective against that character. You also have the option of choosing any other appropriate character in play to capture, but a capture card is generally too valuable to use except to stop or win a battle.

The liability of playing these cards is that they generally add another character card (that would be available for an opponent to rescue) into your Land of Bondage. A character imprisoned in the Land of Bondage is not technically a Lost Soul, but is only treated as Lost Soul. This means that only a card which can affect a Lost Soul will now be able to affect that character.

Net
Snare
Stocks

Result: Immediately capture any Hero and place that Hero into your Land of Bondage.

You may want to wait until you have **Burial** or **Son of God** in your hand before you take a Hero prisoner and place in your own Land of Bondage.

Dungeon of Malchiah

Result: Immediately capture any Hero and place that Hero into an opponent's Land of Bondage.

Not only does this card stop a rescue, but **Dungeon of Malchiah** actually sends a Hero into an opponent's Land of Bondage giving you (or any other player) another available Lost Soul to rescue. What a great card!

Baggage

Result: Immediately capture any Evil Character and place that Evil Character into your Land of Bondage.

This card effectively wins a battle by removing the only blocking Evil Character from the field of battle. You may want to wait until you have **Burial** or **Son of God** in your hand before you take an Evil Character prisoner in your own Land of Bondage.

IGNORE CARDS

When you play an ignore card on a Hero card, the Hero is protected from being directly damaged, affected, or defeated by any Evil Character or enhancement from the color brigade or card type specified by the ignore card.

When you play an ignore card, you will successfully win the battle unless your opponent can play an enhancement card (such as **Rage** or **Ram with Two Horns**) which would introduce an Evil Character from a different color brigade to block the Hero. Your opponent may still play enhancement cards on an Evil Character that is being ignored in order to affect other characters in play.

If banding is not initiated, both characters are returned to their owner's territory at the end of the battle; neither is discarded because no damage is actually dealt.

Ignore Card or Card Type

Stone Cut without Hands
Brass Serpent
Antidote

Result: Allows the Hero upon which it is played to be protected until the end of battle from being directly damaged, affected, or defeated by named cards.

When you play one of these cards, the Hero upon which it is played effectively ignores **Poison** and **Bad Figs** or **Great Image** (as specified) cards for this turn.

The **Stone Cut Without Hands** card is only good for one thing, but if your opponent is playing with the Crimson Brigade, you can be ready for **Great Image** by holding **Stone Cut without Hands**, a Green Brigade Hero, and a banding card in your hand.

Ignore Brigade Cards

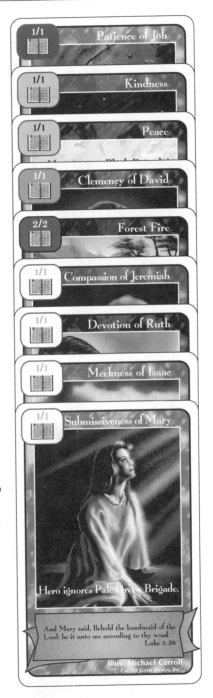

Patience of Job
Kindness
Peace
Clemency of David
Forest Fire
Compassion of Jeremiah
Devotion of Ruth
Meekness of Isaac
Submissiveness of Mary

Result: The Hero upon whom you play the ignore card is protected until the end of battle from being directly damaged, affected, or defeated by any Evil Character or enhancement from a specific color brigade.

Sometimes you can guess which Evil Character will block, and you will be ready with the right ignore card. You may need to use a banding card or **Wheel within a Wheel** to bring in the needed brigade Hero upon whom to play an ignore card.

REPEL CARDS

When you play a repel card on an Evil Character card, then that Evil Character is protected from being directly damaged, affected, or defeated by any Hero or enhancement from the color brigade or card type specified by that ignore card. A repel card will only protect the Evil Character upon which it has been played.

When you play a repel card, you will successfully block the rescue attempt (or win a battle challenge) unless your opponent can play an enhancement card (such as **Sound the Alarm** or **Ezekiel's Stick**) which would introduce a Hero from a different color brigade to continue fighting the battle. Only a Hero and enhancement cards that are of a different color brigade or card type from that being repelled, can have any effect on the battle. Your opponent may still play enhancement cards on the Hero being repelled in order to affect other cards in play.

You may generally think of a repel card as allowing no harm to come to an Evil Character who cunningly out-maneuvers a Hero. The Repel card allows a particular Evil Character to repel any direct effects from the card being ignored but does not necessarily end the battle or prevent any other actions from occurring during a rescue attempt or battle challenge. After the battle both characters are returned to their owner's territory, and neither is discarded because no damage is actually dealt.

Repel Card or Card Type

Delilah
Prince of Persia

Result: This Evil Character is protected from being directly damaged, affected, or defeated by a particular card.

These characters have an innate special ability that repels a particular effect. **Delilah** has a constant repel ability when confronting **Samson**. **Prince of Persia** has the constant ability to repel the **Angel of the Lord** card, unless **Daniel** is actually in the field of battle.

The special abilities of these cards have a limited use, but if you can use them at the right time, they will be just as good as any other stopper.

False Prophesy

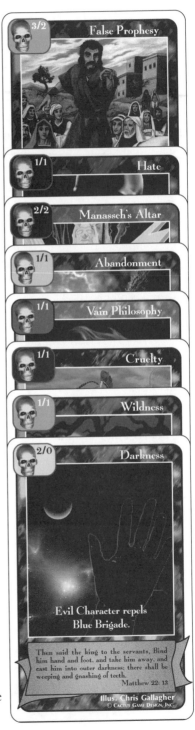

The **False Prophesy** card has created a great deal of discussion of what a prophet is and which characters can be considered to be prophets and which ones are not prophets.

Note: In the Biblical tradition, the word translated as prophet (nabi) means "one who speaks for God" or "God's messenger." By this definition many of the Heroes in the game could be considered to be prophets. You may have to do some research, but any person in the Bible who is actually referred to as being a prophet (or prophetess) should be considered to be a prophet for this game. Therefore, a non-prophet would be a character which is not referred to in the Bible as being a prophet. In this situation Prophets are not exclusive to the Prophets Expansion Set.

Repel Brigade Cards

Hate
Manasseh's Altar
Abandonment
Vain Philosophy
Cruelty
Wildness
Darkness

Result: The Evil Character upon whom you play this card is protected until the end of battle from being directly damaged, affected, or defeated by any Hero or enhancement from the color brigade specified by that repel card.

When a Hero enters the field of battle, you may want to block with an Evil Character card from a brigade for which you have an appropriate repel card. You may need to use a banding card or **False Peace** to bring in the needed Evil Character card upon which to play a repel card.

SET-ASIDE CARDS

Set-aside cards are used to increase the strength and toughness of a character. Characters may be set aside from the player's hand (technically the character is thought of as being played first, then the set-aside card is played on the character), territory, or field of battle, unless otherwise stated on the card. When the character is in the set-aside area, the character increases in offensive strength and defensive toughness by the amount stated on the card. Some set-aside cards require characters to be set aside for a specified number of turns. Others provide an increase of 1/1 for each turn that a character is set aside. Set-aside cards are discarded when a character is returned to the field of play.

It is helpful to use some sort of counter or marker to keep track of the number of turns a character is set aside. A character card has to be in the set-aside area for a complete turn before it gains an increase. If the card is set aside during another player's turn, the set-aside character does not receive a counter until the upkeep phase of your turn following your next turn. A counter is added during your upkeep phase.

A character that is in a set-aside area may be brought back into play any time during your own turn and may be used in battle during that same turn. Set-aside cards are most effective when used in the early stages of a game so that a character's abilities can increase significantly before being brought back into the field of play.

You may also play a set-aside card to save a Hero or Evil Character who is losing in battle and is about to be discarded. You will lose any enhancement cards already played, but you will keep your character from being discarded.

You may not do this with **The Vineyard** because it states that the holder may set aside all Purple Brigade Heroes "in his territory". Cards in the field of battle are outside of a player's territory.

When you set aside an Evil Character during a battle (which does not happen during your turn), the first counter is not placed on the card until the upkeep phase of the turn following your next turn.

Hero Set-aside cards

Iron Pan
Prayer and Fasting
Chastisement of the Lord
Sleep
Meditation
Potter and the Clay
Charred Vine
The Vineyard

Result: The Hero (or Heroes) is immediately sent to a set-aside area to gain an increase in strength and toughness as determined by the instructions on the set-aside card.

Evil Character Set-aside cards

Molech Worship
Covenant with Death
Large Tree
Molten Calf Worship

Result: The Evil Character is immediately sent to a set-aside area to gain an increase in strength and toughness as determined by the instructions on the set-aside card.

BANDING CARDS

Each banding card you play allows an additional character to join in the battle. Characters who join together in the field of battle are treated as a combined force for dealing and receiving damage. Heroes may only band with Heroes. Evil Characters may only band with Evil Characters.

There are general and brigade specific banding cards. Some cards are limited to only being able to add another character from a specified brigade to the battle.

If a banding card is discarded during play, the second character which has been added to the fight may still remain in the field of battle since **the banding card is not what is keeping the extra character in the field of battle—it is only what has allowed the character to join the battle.**

When the character card upon which a banding card has been played is removed from play, all of its enhancement cards are also discarded. The exception to this rule is when the removed character is of the same color as the remaining character, the enhancements cards may be passed to the remaining character. A second character may then be added to replace the discarded character.

When battling against banded characters from two different brigades, be sure to discard the character that is of the same brigade as the banding card to keep another character from joining the battle.

When rescuing, if you plan on using more than one banding card, be careful of the order in which they are played. Some banding cards only allow a second character to join the battle. To play the card **River Flowing from the Temple**, you must have a Hero in your hand.

The evil banding cards are played in the same way that Hero banding cards are played, but there is a limitation on each card. **Rage** bands only 6/6 (or weaker) Evil Characters. **Den of Robbers** and **Ram with Two Horns** can only add a second Evil Character to the battle from the either the Gold or Black Brigades.

Hero Banding Cards

Sound the Alarm
Ezekiel's Stick
Two Olive Branches
River Flowing from the Temple

Result: Holder may add a second Hero to the fight for one turn.

Evil Character Banding

Den of Robbers
Rage
Ram with Two Horns

Result: A second Evil Character joins the battle for one turn.

PREVENT CARDS

A prevent card simply prevents your opponent from playing in a particular way or at a particular time. Prevent cards may affect characters, other enhancements or even the order of play.

False Dreams

Result: The next player may not make a rescue attempt on his next turn, but does not actually lose a turn.

Be careful when you play this card in a two-player game because you are the next player and will not be allowed to attempt a rescue. However, here is how to make two rescue attempts in a row in a two-player game. First, during your turn, play **Cup of Wrath** on a Blue Brigade Hero, then send in one of your own Gray Brigade Evil Characters to battle the Evil Character your opponent is using to block. Next, play **False Dreams**. As it is your turn, the next player would be your opponent and would not be able to make a rescue attempt during his next turn.

Wall Of Fire

Result: Prevents any card in the Black or Pale Green Brigade from having any effect on the rescue attempt.

When you play this card, an opponent cannot play any card from the two stated brigades during this rescue attempt. Black and Pale Green Evil Characters in the field of battle must return to the owner's territory, and evil enhancement cards already played must be discarded. This is a winner when played against a Black or Pale Green Brigade character!

Torn Mantle
Four Horns

Result: Prevent good banding cards from being played this turn and discard any already in play.

To be most effective, you want to play this card before a banding card is even played because once a Hero is already in the field of battle, that Hero is not discarded when the banding card is. Once the prevent banding card has been played, its effects remain active until the end of the turn, even if the card is discarded.

Baal Worship

Result: Evil Characters may not repent this turn.

Baal Worship will stop the **Repentance** card, but this card must be played before the **Repentance** card is played. **Baal Worship** is a prevent card, not a reversal card.

You must anticipate that your opponent might be able to play **Repentance** when you block with a human Evil Character. If your opponent is playing Green Brigade, be ready. If your opponent is playing Heroes with low toughness abilities, then you might have trouble getting the chance to even play **Baal Worship** since there are no Evil Characters in the Crimson Brigade with a toughness lower than six.

EXCHANGE CARDS

Exchange cards allow you to exchange one card during play for another. This ability can suddenly confound your opponent's strategy and perhaps leave him without a sufficient way to block or win a rescue attempt.

Lion Dwelling With the Calf

Result: Your opponent must exchange the current blocking Evil Character with a new blocker.

If your opponent cannot produce a different blocker from his territory or hand, then the rescue is successful. The Evil Character which refuses to block is returned to the owner's territory and any enhancement cards which have been played on it are discarded. If your opponent makes the exchange from the same color brigade, then the enhancement cards already played will be retained by (or passed to) the new character in the battle. This is a great card to play when you know that your opponent only has one Evil Character or you would rather battle a different character or brigade. Playing this card on the turn after **Plague of Flies** or **Authority of Christ** or early in the game might just win you an easy rescue.

Wheel Within a Wheel

Result: Holder exchanges the current Hero in the field of battle with a different Hero from his own draw pile and continues to play.

This card is useful to exchange your current rescuing Hero for a stronger Hero, a Hero from a brigade for which you have a banding or other strong enhancement card in your hand, or when your current color brigade has been repelled. You will have to reshuffle your deck after the exchange, but you have had the opportunity to remind yourself of the cards that are still available in your draw pile.

Obedience of Noah
Lies

Result: Exchanges the character your opponent has in the field of battle with another character.

When your opponent has played a character that you know will be difficult to defeat, you can simply select a different character which your opponent will have to use and return the original character to his own territory. The character selected can come from any territory in the field of play or from your hand. Your opponent will control the new character for this turn. If the character should survive, it is returned to its owner's field of play. If the character is discarded, it should be sent to the owner's discard pile.

It is most effective to select a character from your hand or from any player's territory that is of a color brigade which your opponent does not have in his deck. In a multi-player game your opponent can always ask for help. In a multi-player game be careful to follow the "holder" and "owner" terminology in the instructions on these cards, for this will determine who actually selects the new character card used.

It would be a good time to play one of these cards after your opponent has played several enhancements. Unless you select a new character of the same color brigade, all of your opponent's enhancement cards in the field of battle are discarded.

WITHDRAWAL CARDS

These cards allow you to make an honorable retreat when your character is losing the battle. Not only does your character survive and return to your territory, but any enhancements you have played are also returned to your hand so you can use them again later.

Highway
Stillness

Result: Hero may withdraw to the owner's territory unharmed. All enhancement cards played may be returned to the player's hand except for the withdrawal card itself.

Withdrawing from a battle may be advantageous when your character is about to lose the battle or when your opponent has made a surprise play which confounds your strategy.

You may also withdraw when your Hero is about to win a battle so you can save any enhancement cards for another turn, but a Lost Soul will not be rescued.

When played, withdrawal cards end the battle. These cards may not be played after a rescue has been successfully completed.

When you play a withdrawal card, you may save the enhancement cards you played during this battle, but your opponent may not. Your opponent must discard any enhancement cards played while blocking the rescue attempt. This strategy will make your opponent weaker in that color brigade during later rescue attempts.

FIRST-STRIKE CARDS

The first-strike cards give the character the ability to deal all damage before the other character has a chance to deal any damage. This would enable the character with the first-strike advantage to survive a battle which would otherwise end in the mutual destruction of both characters.

David's Sling
Pillar of a Cloud
Speed

Result: Hero deals damage before the opposing character can deal any damage.

Because damage is dealt simultaneously, in a mutual destruction situation a Hero would normally be discarded, but would still win a Lost Soul. Having the first-strike ability in this situation will allow the Hero to survive and still win the Lost Soul. But if the Hero is not strong enough to reduce the Evil Character's toughness to 0 or below, then striking first does not make any difference in a battle.

REDUCTION CARDS

These cards temporarily weaken the strength and toughness of other characters. Some of these cards will affect more than one target. The effects last until the end of the turn so don't place a character card with a low toughness into your territory during your discard phase if it will still be affected enough to be sent to the discard pile.

Filthy Garments
Hunger
Ignorance
Plague of Flies

Result: Immediately weakens specified character(s) for the rest of turn.

When you play these cards, you reduce the abilities of specified characters seriously weakening their ability to win a battle. If the reduction causes a character's toughness to fall to zero or below, the character must be discarded at the end of the battle.

Hunger and **Ignorance** are good defenses against banded Heroes because they affect all your opponents Heroes simultaneously. **Plague of Flies** works especially well against banded Evil Characters and really gives a Hero a good chance to win by the numbers against some of the most powerful Evil Characters. You might want to play **Hunger** or **Ignorance** on the turn right after **Valley of Dry Bones** has returned all Heroes to players territories.

Filthy Garments affects one Hero. **Hunger** affects all of the Heroes of one opponent. **Ignorance** affects all Heroes in play, including your own. **Plague of Flies** affects all Evil Characters in play, including your own.

AMPLIFY CARDS

An amplify card increases or amplifies a character's own abilities. The amount of the increase will be different when played on different characters.

The Branch

Result: Gives a male character from the Purple Brigade an increase in strength and toughness for this turn.

This temporary increase in a Hero's abilities may be just enough to win the battle. This card would give an increase of 3/3 to **Jonathan**, or an increase of 3.5/2.5 to **Elisha**. This card does not amplify the value of any other enhancement cards, nor does it amplify any increases from being set aside or healed.

Vain Vision
Woman in the Ephah

Result: When played against certain Heroes, the abilities of a character are amplified.

When played against specified opponents, these cards gain abilities greater than their face amounts.

When blocking a Red Brigade Hero, **Woman in the Ephah** is stronger than **Goat with Horn**, otherwise they have the same value. When playing **Vain Vision** against a prophet, its abilities double.

CHALLENGE CARDS

A challenge card immediately interrupts play and requires two Evil Characters to battle. After the battle is resolved, if the initial blocking Evil Character was the victor, the rescue attempt continues. If the challenging Evil Character is successful, the rescue is accomplished; the original blocking character and all enhancement cards are discarded, and the victorious characters are returned to their owner's territory.

Cup of Wrath

Result: The holder chooses two Evil Characters in play to battle each other, temporarily interrupting the initial battle.

This card gives you the opportunity to have another Evil Character try to defeat a blocker. You may choose any Evil Character in play regardless of who owns the card. The owner plays enhancement cards as if it were a normal battle. If the original blocker wins, then all enhancements played remain in play during the remainder of the rescue attempt.

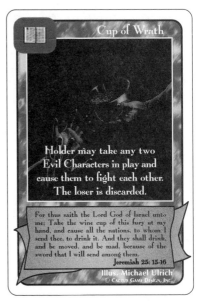

You don't have to choose the initial blocker for the battle; you may select any two Evil Characters to remove one of them from the game. **Cup of Wrath** is one of the Blue Brigade's best chances of winning a battle. Therefore, not using it to defeat a blocker may not be the best use of the card.

It can be risky to invite another Evil Character into the field of battle. Although it is between two Evil Characters, some of the enhancement cards may affect you. If a capture or return card is played, your original battle may be lost. If a player is using this card to assist another player during an optional advanced rules, multi-player game, the "holder" of the card chooses the Evil Characters that fight.

SEEK AND FIND CARDS

A seek and find card allows you to find out some secret information by looking through a deck or at the cards in a player's hand. What a great advantage when you are trying to decide what kind of strategy to use!

False Peace

Result: Look through your own deck and select a card to add to your hand.

With **False Peace** you can select **Christian Martyr, Snare, Chains**, or any other card to use in the battle. You could find any card in your deck and have it in your hand when you need it. If both you and your opponent have four Redeemed Souls and you are losing the battle, play this card to find your **Son of God** card (if it hasn't been drawn already) and instantly rescue a fifth Lost Soul to win the game.

Another advantage with this card is the opportunity to check out what cards you have left in your draw pile which could be very helpful late in the game. You have to reshuffle the draw pile after you look through it, but just knowing your options might help you plan your strategy. (About a minute should be long enough for a player to search through his draw pile and choose a card in this situation.)

False Wisdom

Result: Look at the cards in the rescuer's hand.

False Wisdom enables you to see what cards your opponent has to play during this rescue attempt. Knowing you can win the battle will certainly help you know whether to continue playing enhancement cards or whether that would be just a waste of your resources.

It is advantageous to learn what cards your opponent has to use against you when it comes time for him or her to block during your next turn. You will know what to play for the best chance of winning the battle.

Confusion

Result: Player chooses any card and discards it from the draw pile of one opponent.

Playing this card allows you to discard a powerful instant card (**Son of God, Burial, Angel of the Lord**) or any other card (**Authority of Christ, Ignorance, Aaron's Rod, Furnace of God's Wrath**) which would be particularly troublesome to your deck. One great advantage of this card is the opportunity to look at all of the cards in the draw pile of your opponent. It is only fair to set a time limit (about a minute) for how long you may look through a draw pile before you choose a card to discard.

THE LOST SOULS CARD

Result: This card counts as two Lost Souls, and must be rescued twice.

For customizing your play deck, this card counts as a single card when counting the number of Lost Soul cards.

Because there are special instructions written on the face of the card, you are only allowed to have one **Lost Souls** card for every 50 in the deck. This means that if you have 50 to 99 cards in your deck, you can only have only one **Lost Souls** card. If you have 100 to 149 cards in your deck, you may have two **Lost Souls** cards.

During the game, two rescues must be successful before either of the **Lost Souls** card Redeemed Souls count toward winning the game.

To nullify an opponent's rescue (of the first of the two Lost Souls), play **Burial** on the **Lost Souls** card after the first rescue. The limited edition **Lost Souls** card may be rescued by two different players, with each player getting credit for one rescue. The unlimited edition **Lost Souls** card must be rescued twice by the same player before either rescue can be counted; except that the second Lost Soul may be rescued by another player using the **Son of God** card. In the final turns of the game, if your opponent has four Redeemed Souls and successfully completes a fifth rescue, if possible, choose the first Lost Soul of a **Lost Souls** card in your Land of Bondage as being rescued. Because both Lost Souls have to be rescued for a player to receive credit for either one, this move will actually make that player have to rescue a sixth Lost Soul in order to win the game.

Sample Game Using Basic Decks

David and Laurie are the two players in this sample game which will demon-strate many of the ways in which cards are strategically played. Additional dia-logue is added to explain the actions of each player. The words in italics describe the special ability printed on a card. Characters which survive in battle should be understood to be returned to the owner's territory after a battle. Both decks are from the starter set of the limited edition. David is playing the A deck and Laurie is playing the B deck.

David and Laurie shuffle their own decks and then cut each other's decks. Laurie flips a coin to see who goes first. David wins the coin toss. Both David and Laurie draw eight cards each from their decks.

David draws **Uriah, Steadfastness of Peter, Bow and Arrow**, Lost Soul, Lost Soul, **Lance, Darkness** and **Angel of the Lord**. Since David drew two Lost Souls he places them in his Land of Bondage and pulls two more cards from his draw pile. He draws **Grief**, and **David's Staff**.

Laurie draws **Shield of Faith**, Lost Soul; **Locust from the Pit, Faith, Courage, Lost Soul, Shimei**, and **Judas Iscariot**. Since she drew two Lost Souls, she places them in her Land of Bondage and draws two replacement cards from her draw pile. She draws **Ruth**, and **Ezekiel's Stick**.

David: So, I go first. I don't draw on the first turn, so I'll make a rescue attempt with **Uriah** (6/6 Red Hero).

Laurie: I'll defend with **Shimei** (6/6 Brown Evil Character).

David: Then, I'll enhance **Uriah** with **Bow and Arrow** (2/1 Red Hero enhancement). What else have you got?

Laurie: Looks like I have one less Lost Soul in my Land of Bondage. (Laurie discards **Shimei** and places one Lost Soul into David's Land of Redemption. David discards his enhancement.) Is it my turn?

David: Yes.

(next turn)

Laurie: Let's see, I don't draw on my first turn either, so I'll make a rescue attempt with **Ruth** (4/4 White Hero).

David: (David hands Laurie a Lost Soul from his Land of Bondage.)

Laurie: What, no defense? I guess it's your turn then.

(next turn)

David: I draw three cards (**Task Master, Gideon**, Lost Soul). I drew a Lost Soul, so I'll put it in the Land of Bondage and draw another (**Miriam**). I'll make a rescue attempt with **Uriah** (6/6 Red Hero) again.

Laurie: I'll block with **Judas Iscariot** (6/6 Crimson Evil Character).

David: I'll enhance with **David's Staff** (2/2 Red Hero enhancement). My 8/8 to your 6/6. (Laurie hands David a Lost Soul.) I only have eight cards in my hand, so it's your turn.

(next turn)

Laurie: I draw three cards (**Barnabas**, Lost Soul, Lost Soul). Two Lost Souls! Woe is me. I'll replace them with two cards from my draw pile (**Balm of Gilead, Stone Throwers**). **Barnabas** will attempt a rescue.

David: I'll block with **Task Master** (6/6 Gold Evil Character).

Laurie: Fair enough, I'll enhance with **Courage** (2/2 Blue Hero enhancement). Now I'm 6/6.

David: Let's put a little **Grief** (2/2 Gold evil enhancement) into the situation. I'm 8/8.

Laurie: It's so sad, but **Faith** (2/2 Blue Hero enhancement) is the answer to **Grief**. Now **Barnabas** is 8/8 and we're in a mutual destruction situation.

David: Okay, you'll win the Lost Soul; but, if you don't enhance you'll lose **Barnabas**, no matter how much **Faith** and **Courage** he has.

Laurie: Ah, but there is a Balm in Gilead that can heal the grief torn soul. I'll heal **Barnabas** with **Balm of Gilead** (Blue Hero enhancement, *Heal any Hero from the Blue Brigade that is being discarded.*) (Laurie and David discard all enhancements, David discards **Task Master**. **Barnabas** returns to Laurie's territory. David hands Laurie a Lost Soul.)

(next turn)

David: I draw three cards (**Doeg**, Lost Soul, **Stone of Thebez**). I drew a Lost Soul, so I'll replace it with another draw (**Helmet of Salvation**). I'll attempt a rescue with **Gideon**.

Laurie: I'll block with **Stone Throwers** (6/6 Crimson Evil Character).

David: I'll take this opportunity to play **Angel of the Lord** (Lamb icon card, *Discard any Evil Character in play.*) (Laurie discards **Stone Throwers** and gives David a Lost Soul.)

(next turn)

Laurie: I draw three cards (**Christian Martyr, Esther, Helmet of Salvation**). I'll make a rescue attempt with **Esther** (6/6 Purple Hero).

David: **Esther!** I'll block with **Doeg**, (6/6 Pale Green evil enhancement).

Laurie: I'll enhance **Esther** with **Ezekiel's Stick** which will bring **Barnabas** into the battle. Now I'm 10/10.

David: Okay, I'll enhance **Doeg** with **Darkness** (2/0, Pale Green enhancement, *Evil Character repels Blue Brigade.*) Now, I'm 8/6 and you're back down to 6/6.

Laurie: I'll enhance **Esther** with the **Helmet of Salvation** (0/4, multi-colored Hero enhancement), then she'll be 6/10.

David: Then I'll play **Lance** (2/2 Pale Green evil enhancement) bringing **Doeg** to 10/8.

Laurie: Wow...let's see here. If I play **Shield of Faith** (0/4 multi-colored Hero enhancement), then **Esther** will be 6/14. I believe that puts us in a stalemate. Do you have any more enhancements?

David: Well, I'll...uh...pass. Do you have any enhancements?

Laurie: I'll pass also, because Pale Green only has 3 cards in the starter deck. Unless you have added some enhancements, we'll have to call this a stalemate and both disengage.

David: I retire, if you do.

Laurie: I retire.

(Both David and Laurie disengage their characters from battle and discard all enhancements.)

(next turn)

David: Okay, my turn. I'll draw three cards (**Herodias, Peace, Samuel**). I'll make a rescue attempt with **Samuel** (4/4 gold Hero).

Laurie: Okay, I'll block with **Locust from the Pit** (6/6, Black Brigade Evil Character). Since you're losing this battle, you add the first enhancement.

David: I know...I'll place **Peace** on my Hero (1/1, Gold Hero Enhancement, *Hero ignores Black Brigade.*). Read it and weep.

Laurie: Ignore Black! I'm glad you only have one of those. I guess you'd win a Lost Soul if I didn't have this **Christian Martyr** (grim reaper icon, *Discard any Hero in play.*).

David: Ah, foiled again. (**Samuel** and **Peace** are discarded. **Christian Martyr** is discarded. **Locust from the Pit** returns to Laurie's territory.)

David: I have fewer than eight cards in my hand, your turn.

(next turn)

Laurie: Okay, I'll draw three cards (**Jezebel, Pillar of a Cloud, Chariots of Iron**). I'll put **Esther** (6/6 Purple Hero) in for a rescue attempt.

David: I'll block with **Herodias** (6/6, Gold Evil Character). I think you get the first enhancement since we're tied.

Laurie: Right. I'll place **Pillar of a Cloud** (2/2 multi-colored enhancement, *Hero gains first strike ability for the turn.*) on **Esther**. What have you got?

David: I'll enhance **Herodias** with the **Stone of Thebez** (2/2, Gold evil enhancement). The battle is tied again, have you any more enhancements?

Laurie: Did you notice that **Pillar of a Cloud** gives **Esther** first-strike capability? Therefore I'm winning, and you go next.

David: Good play. I don't think that I can beat that. Here's your Lost Soul.

Laurie: Redeemed Soul, you mean. I'll just place her in my Land of Redemption if you don't mind. (David discards **Herodias** and the enhancement card. Laurie discards her enhancement card and returns **Esther** to her Territory.) It's your turn.

(next turn)

David: I draw three (**Christian Martyr, Wisdom, Prayer and Fasting**) Wow!! lucky draw. I'll make a rescue attempt with **Gideon** (6/6, Gold Hero).

Laurie: Okay, I'll block with **Jezebel** (6/6, Crimson Evil Character).

David: I get to add the first enhancement, so I'll enhance with **Wisdom** (2/2 Gold Hero enhancement). I'm 8/8, what do you have?

Laurie: I will enhance **Jezebel** with **Chariots of Iron** (2/2 Crimson evil enhancement). That makes her 8/8. Any more?

David: We're in a mutual destruction situation, unless you have any more enhancements, I win the Lost Soul.

Laurie: Okay, I confess, I don't have anything else to enhance with. You win the Lost Soul. But unless you have something else to enhance with, you'll lose your Hero.

David: Just watch me. I'll play **Prayer and Fasting** (*Set Hero aside. Hero gains 1/1 for every turn Hero prays.*) to set my **Gideon** aside.

Laurie: Wait a minute! You can't do that.

David: When a character is losing you can heal or set aside to keep the character from being discarded.

Laurie: That is true. But you aren't really losing in a mutual destruction situation once damage is dealt, you actually have won the battle. Once the battle is over you can't play an enhancement. A set-aside or healing card would have to be played before damage is dealt, so in this case if you had set **Gideon** aside, you would not win the Lost Soul because your Hero would no longer be in the field of battle at the end of the battle.

David: Hey, you know what, you're right about that. Where did you learn how to play so well?

Laurie: I bought a copy of the *Redemption*™ Player's Guide.

David: Great commercial. (**Gideon** is placed on top of the discard pile and **Prayer and Fasting** returns to his hand since he was not allowed to play it. David discards his **Wisdom** enhancement. Laurie discards **Jezebel** and the enhancement. Laurie gives David a Lost Soul.) Your turn.

(next turn)

Laurie: I draw three (**Son of God**, **Net**, Lost Soul). I drew a Lost Soul, so I'll place it in my Land of Bondage and draw again (**Strength**). I'll make a rescue attempt with **Barnabas** (4/4 Blue Hero).

David: I'll use my **Christian Martyr** (grim reaper icon, *Discard any Hero in play.*) card to discard your Hero. (David discards his **Christian Martyr** card and sends **Barnabas** to the top of Laurie's discard pile.)

Laurie: Hey! That doesn't seem fair!

David: That's what the card was created for.

(next turn)

David: Okay, I'll draw three cards (**Chains, Sound the Alarm, Clemency of David**) Sorry, no Lost Soul. If I had been able to set **Gideon** aside, he would be stronger now and be too powerful for your weakened defenses this late in the game. I'll make a rescue attempt with **Uriah** (6/6 Red Hero).

Laurie: I'll defend with **Locust from the Pit** (6/6 Black Evil Character).

David: I'll enhance with **Sound the Alarm** (*Holder may add a second Hero to the fight for one turn.*), which allows me to add **Miriam** (4/4 Green Hero) to the fight. Now I'm 10/10.

Laurie: Hmm...I'll enhance my blocker with **Net** (2/2 black evil enhancement, *Take any Hero prisoner and place Hero in your Land of Bondage. Hero is treated as a Lost Soul.*) to capture **Uriah** and place him in my Land of Bondage. Now, my so called "weak" defender is blocking at 8/8. I believe you're back to 4/4.

David: Ouch, that hurt. (Laurie places **Uriah** in her Land of Bondage and discards **Net**. David discards the **Miriam** and **Sound the Alarm** cards.)

(next turn)

Laurie: My turn? I draw three cards (**Mercy of James, Poison, Obedience of Noah**). It is your turn. (Laurie is not confident that she can make a successful fourth rescue this turn. She decides to wait for the next turn as she has decided to save the **Son of God** card for her fifth rescue.)

(next turn)

David: I'll draw three cards (Lost Soul, **Faithful Servant, False Teachers**). I drew a Lost Soul, so I'll draw a replacement (**Ointment**). I'll make a rescue attempt with **Faithful Servant** (4/4 Green Hero).

Laurie: I'll block with **Locust from the Pit** (6/6 Black Evil Character).

David: Oh, I was hoping you'd be out of Black Brigade enhancements and use another character.

Laurie: Why, do you have an ignore card?

David: I'll enhance with **Ointment** (0/2, Green Hero enhancement). And since I'm still losing the battle, I'll enhance with **Clemency of David** (1/1, green Hero enhancement, *Hero ignores Brown Brigade.*). That makes **Faithful Servant** 5/7 and puts us in a stalemate. You go next.

Laurie: So you did have an ignore card. I can live with a stalemate. Do you retire or do you have other enhancements?

David: Well, I'll retire if you do. (David discards his two enhancements and both characters return to their territories.)

(next turn)

Laurie: Great! I draw three cards (**Silas, Axe, Devotion of Ruth**). I'll make a rescue attempt with **Silas** (4/4 Blue Hero).

David: I'll block with **False Teachers** (6/6 Gray Evil Character).

Laurie: Watch this…I'll enhance **Silas** with **Obedience of Noah** (1/1 Blue Hero enhancement, *Holder may choose the Evil Character that his opponent uses to block his rescue attempt.*). I choose that you block with **Locust from the Pit**.

David: But that's your Evil Character.

Laurie: That's right, and I'm sure you don't have any black evil enhancements. Now I'll add **Strength** (3/3, Blue Hero enhancement) to **Silas** and I believe that 7/7 wins the battle.

David: Here's your Lost Soul. That ties us four to four.

Laurie: Well, it would, except that I am now going to play my **Son of God** (lamb icon, *Rescue any Lost Soul in play.*) card and rescue a fifth Lost Soul from my own Land of Bondage. That's the game.

David: That really was a great game! How about playing best two out of three?

DECK BUILDING

One of the most enjoyable aspects of *Redemption™* is deck building. You choose the cards which will join together as the Army of God to rescue Lost Souls. You also choose the evil forces which will defend your Land of Bondage. You may think of a deck you built as a customized, tuned, or theme deck. Be creative when customizing your own deck and even give your deck a name if you want to.

It is a good idea to keep track of:
1) Which cards you use in a deck.
2) How many games you win with that deck.
3) What the basic strengths and weaknesses of that deck are.

The order in which cards are drawn adds a random factor to the game. You may have built a much better deck than your opponent, but the draw may not be working in your favor during any given game. If you draw several Lost Souls in the first couple of rounds and your opponent only draws one, then you will have a difficult time defending your Land of Bondage for the entire game. You will also be forced to discard many useful cards during your discard phase.

NUMBER OF CARDS

You will need to decide how many cards you want to use in your deck. Try playing a small deck containing as few Lost Souls as possible, using only one or two colors from each army. You will be more likely to draw the matching enhancement cards to play with your characters. You probably need to use as many as seven Heroes and up to ten enhancements cards for your major color and fewer for the supporting brigades.

Playing a deck of 100 cards will allow you to include two of each of the powerful special ability cards that are winners and stoppers, but you will not be assured of drawing the more powerful cards early enough in the game to help you win. A large deck also reduces your chances of drawing the four specialty cards during the game.

BALANCING YOUR DECK

You will need to balance the number of characters and enhancement cards of each brigade you keep in your deck. If you do not include enough characters in your deck, then you will not be able to effectively use your enhancement cards. Your lonely enhancement cards will take up space in your hand or you will discard them before they can be played. If you do not include enough enhancement cards, you leave your characters vulnerable in battle or stranded in their own territory without any help from their own brigades.

You will need to decide how many brigades to keep in your deck. The fewer brigades you use, the greater the odds that the enhancement cards in your hand will match your color brigades. Playing one brigade from each army means that you will nearly always be able to play enhancement cards, but you will have a smaller ratio of the winners and stoppers. The more brigades you use, the more winners and stoppers you can pack into your deck, but the odds will also be less favorable that you will have the right characters in play to match those enhancements. A deck that has many colors in it is slower to develop, but has more potential to win a long game.

THE RANDOM FACTOR

Since players cannot choose the cards they want to play from their draw piles, there is a random factor in the game. You can plan your deck to avoid being unnecessarily penalized by this randomness. Because the Specialty cards are so powerful, you will want to know the probability of drawing one of your four Specialty cards in your initial draw of eight cards. In a 56 card deck you will have a 47.2% chance of drawing one of those four Specialty cards in the opening draw. If you have a 69 card deck, you will have a 39.8% probability of drawing one of those Specialty cards in the opening draw. If you have a 100 card deck, the probability of drawing one of those Specialty cards in the opening draw drops to 28.8%. Therefore, the more cards your deck contains, the lower the probability of actually getting to play these cards during the game.

WINNERS AND STOPPERS

You will want to use as many cards as possible in your deck that will immediately win or stop a battle. Cards like **Authority of Christ** and **Furnace of God's Wrath** are winners. Most capture and return cards are stoppers. Most brigades only contain one or two winners or stoppers. Because some cards like banding cards allow you to gain temporary control of another player's character for a turn, you might want to include some of the winners and stoppers (to use as a surprise) from brigades that you don't keep in your deck.

BUILDING YOUR DECK

A deck of 56 cards will contain seven Lost Soul cards. You will want to put in the four Specialty cards. You might want to include some power enhancement cards such as **Shoes of Peace, Pillar of a Cloud,** and **Sun Worship** for early battles which might be decided by the numbers. This leaves you with 42 cards to choose. If you want to play with one brigade from each opposing army, then you might want to use nine characters and 12 enhancement cards from each brigade. If you want to play with two brigades from each force, you may include four or five characters from each brigade and then choose the best enhancement cards to fill out your deck. You might play with three good brigades and one evil brigade; then you would still choose four or five characters from each brigades and fill out your deck with the best enhancement cards from those brigades. You cannot actually win the game by having the most powerful evil forces, but you can slow down your opponent. You must have a powerful offensive team to rescue enough Lost Souls to win the game.

All decks must conform to the deck construction rules found in the basic rule book. In addition, the following restrictions apply:

a) no deck may contain more than three of any card with the same name in the same brigade (other than Lost Soul cards)

b) no deck may contain more than one for each 50 of any single card having special instructions written on it (text over the illustration).

*Example: A 56-card deck may contain only one **Authority of Christ**, one **Repentance**, etc.... A 100-card deck may contain no more than two **Authority of Christ** cards, two **Repentance** cards and so on. A 150-card deck may contain no more than three of any individual special ability card.*

EXAMPLES OF CUSTOMIZED DECKS

Try playing with some of these customized decks to learn the strengths and weaknesses of different kinds of decks. There are many special ability cards in these decks. Practice your strategy for putting the best combinations into play. Note: When a (2) appears before a card, then there are two of that individual card in the deck.

Laurie's Royal Warrior Deck (63 cards)

Purple Brigade
Esther
Ezekiel
Elisha
Habakkuk
Jonathan
River Flowing from the Temple
Speed
The Branch
Elisha's Bones
The Vineyard
Ezekiel's Stick
Authority of Christ

Red Brigade
Shamgar
Malachi
Joab
Adino
Uriah
Arrow of Deliverance
Potter and the Clay
Arrow of Deliverance
Wheel within a Wheel
David's Sling
Sound the Alarm
Forest Fire

Black Brigade
(2) Goliath
(2) Shemaiah
Abaddon the Destroyer
Woman in the Ephah

Hunger
Yoke of Iron
Vain Vision
Net

Pale Green Brigade
Beast from the Sea
(2) Doeg
Wizards
Workers with Familiar Spirits
Prince of Persia
Rage
Stocks
Torn Mantle
Filthy Garments
Confusion

Power Enhancement cards
Pillar of a Cloud
Helmet of Salvation
Sword of the Spirit
Breastplate of Righteousness
Shield of Faith
Sun Worship

Lost Soul cards
(7) Lost Soul (1) Lost Souls

Specialty Cards
Son of God
Angel of the Lord
Christian Martyr
Burial

Stuart Whitaker's 100 Card Deck

Red Brigade
Christian Soldier
Asahel
Gad
Shamgar
Malachi
(2) Sound the Alarm
(2) Wheel Within a Wheel
(2) Baggage
(1) Healing
(2) Forest Fire

Green Brigade
Faithful Servant
Zechariah
The Watchman
(2) Isaiah
(2) Repentance
(2) Aaron's Rod
(2) Valley of Dry Bones
(2) Bread of Life
(2) Stone Cut Without Hands
Clemency of David

Gold Brigade
Othniel
Deborah
Huldah
Simeon
Moses
(2) Furnace of God's Wrath
(2) Two Olive Branches
(2) Highway
(2) Plague of Flies
Kindness
Peace

Brown Brigade
Haman
Ahaziah
Delilah
Beast from the Earth
(2) Cage
(2) Paul's Girdle
(2) Dungeon of Malchiah
(2) Ignorance

Gray Brigade
(2) False Prophets
Abihu
Balaam
(2) False Peace
(2) False Dreams
(2) Chains
(2) Snare

Pale Green Brigade
(2) Workers with Familiar Spirits
Prince of Persia
Witch of Endor
(2) Confusion
(2) Rage
(2) Stocks
(2) Torn Mantle
Filthy Garments

Lost Soul cards
(2) Lost Souls
(12) Lost Soul

Specialty Cards
Son of God
Angel of the Lord
Christian Martyr
Burial

John Jackson's Mighty Warrior Tournament Deck (62 cards)

Red Brigade
Mighty Warrior
Malachi
Adino
Shamgar
Joab
Wheel within a Wheel
David's Sling
Potter and the Clay
Sound the Alarm
Baggage
(2) Arrow of Deliverance

Brown Brigade
Beast from the Earth
Ahab
Haman
Enchanter
Delilah
(2) Bad Figs
Paul's Girdle
Ignorance
Boils
Cage

White Brigade
Jeremiah
Ruth
John the Baptist
Daniel
Mary
(3) Mountain of God
Wall of Fire
Submissiveness of Mary
Sleep
Lion Dwelling with the Calf

Black Brigade
Goliath
Abaddon the Destroyer
Locust from the Pit
Manasseh
Damsel with Spirit of Divination
Yoke of Iron
Vain Vision
Woman in the Ephah
Hunger
Manasseh's Altar
Net

Power Enhancement cards
Pillar of a Cloud
Shoes of Peace
Sword of the Spirit
Sun Worship

Specialty cards
Son of God
Angel of the Lord
Burial
Christian Martyr

Lost Soul cards
(8) Lost Soul

Red White & Blue Deck (68 cards)

John Coleman customized this deck for a female friend. The characters are either female or genderless, as are most of the enhancement cards.

White Brigade
(3) Mary
(2) Philip's Daughters
Devotion of Ruth
Wall of Fire
Submissiveness of Mary
Charred Vine
Sleep
(2) Mountain of God
Angel Food

Blue Brigade
(3) Anna
Hannah
(2) Rebekah
(2) Strength
(2) Obedience of Noah (3/3)
Stillness
Iron Pan
Patience of Job
Chastisement of the Lord

Lost Soul cards
(1) Lost Souls (8) Lost Soul

Crimson Brigade
(3) Salome
(3) Jezebel
(2) Whore of Babylon
(2) Red Dragon
(3) Weeping for Tammuz
Covenant with Death
Great Image
Vain Philosophy
Four Horns
(3) First Figs
(2) Fiery Darts
(2) Discord
(2) Treachery
Chariots of Iron

Power Enhancement cards
Pillar of a Cloud
Sword of the Spirit

Specialty Cards
Christian Martyr
Angel of the Lord
Son of God

John Coleman's Day and Night Deck (51 cards)

White Brigade
(2) Daniel
Philip's Daughters
(2) John the Baptist
(2) Jeremiah
Ruth
Mary
(2) Angel Food
(3) Mountain of God
Devotion of Ruth
Charred Vine
Lion Dwelling with the Calf
Submissiveness of Mary
Wall of Fire
Sleep

Power Enhancement Cards
Sword of the Spirit
Pillar of a Cloud
Shoes of Peace
Sun Worship

Black Brigade
(2) Goliath
Abaddon the Destroyer
Locust from the Pit
Prophets of Samaria
(3) Goat with Horn
(2) Goliath's Spear
Hunger
Vain Vision
Manasseh's Altar
Yoke of Iron
Net
Hate

Specialty Cards
Burial
Angel of the Lord
Son of God
Christian Martyr

Lost Soul cards
(6) Lost Soul (1) Lost Souls

David's Deck of Many Colors (56 cards)

Sometimes you just want to have fun. That is what the deck of many colors is all about. Watch the surprised look on your opponent's face as you gradually play characters from all the good brigades in the first few turns. Save back the evil forces as long as possible to keep your opponent from knowing which brigade you have. All of the Heroes have a toughness of four or less to ensure you play the first enhancement card.

When playing in a multi-player game, be sure to use your opponent's strengthened characters as much as possible when you need to win the battle by the numbers. If you really want to surprise someone, don't put any Evil Characters in your deck at all and hope your Lost Soul cards don't come out too quickly. Rescue and bury two of your own Lost Soul cards with your Specialty cards to reduce the Lost Soul cards available to your opponent. Hold a green character in your hand in case all your Heroes are discarded by some terrible evil enhancement card. Then play **Valley of Dry Bones** on the next turn to bring all your Heroes home.

The strength of this deck is in the winners and the ignore cards. This deck is especially tuned against the purple and Green Brigades of Laurie's Royal Warrior Deck. You might want to add in some of the other ignore cards to make the deck more adaptable against other decks.

Blue Brigade
Mark
Rebekah
Silas
Patience of Job
Obedience of Noah

Gold Brigade
Samuel
Othniel
Deborah
Plague of Flies
Furnace of God's Wrath
Peace

Green Brigade
Faithful Servant
Cornelius
Miriam
The Watchman
Valley of Dry Bones
Repentance
Aaron's Rod

Purple Brigade
Ezekiel
Hosea
Habakkuk
Authority of Christ
River Flowing from the Temple
Ezekiel's Stick

Red Brigade
Mighty Warrior
Hushai
Asahel
Christian Soldier
Baggage
Wheel Within a Wheel
Sound the Alarm

White Brigade
Philip's Daughters
John the Baptist
Mary
Wall of Fire
Submissiveness of Mary
Lion Dwelling with the Calf

Gray Brigade
False Prophets
The False Prophet
Balaam
Chaldeans
False Peace
Snare
Chains
False Prophesy

Lost Soul cards
(7) Lost Soul (all Little Boy)

Specialty Cards
Christian Martyr
Burial
Son of God
Angel of the Lord

MULTI-PLAYER GAMES

Playing *Redemption*™ with more than one other person can be tricky, but it is a lot of fun. To win in a multi-player game you will need to practice your strategy, timing, bluffing, and deck building skills. You must also hope that other players don't team up against you all the time, but if you have a reputation for winning this game, then you might as well expect them to! If you don't win very often, then you will learn to play for the beauty of the game and the enjoyment of the fellowship; and you will still gain some victories in the process.

Multi-player games still follow the same rules found in the Basic Rules section. In addition, playing by the Tournament Rules will allow you to join any game without having to decide what optional or "house rules" will apply.

There are a few things to keep in mind when playing a multi-player game:

1) Before the game begins, all players must agree whether to include any optional rule(s).

   Example: Players rescue seven (or even 13) Lost Souls to win the game. Enhancement cards with the name of a character have a double value when played on the character of the same name.

2) When it is decided which player will have the first turn, then the player seated to the left will be the next player to take a turn. Play continues clockwise around the table.

3) Players draw eight cards to form a beginning hand for the first round, then they do not draw again until the beginning of their second turn.

   Hint: If there are four players in the game, and you will be last to draw again, try not to use up your enhancement cards too quickly.

4) Some cards (such as banding cards) allow you to use another player's characters that are in the field of play. This means you might want to include powerful enhancement cards from brigades you do not have in your deck for use when you control another player's characters.

5) Players will need to keep track of who owns which Lost Soul card by placing different counters on the cards. Having many counters in the playing area can be confusing. Another option would be to trade the Lost Soul cards with each other so that each person uses seven (or the proper number) of the same Lost Soul card in his or her deck. If one player had all of the "Woman in Black" Lost Soul cards in the game it would be easier to return them at the end of the game. *Rob Anderson uses all ("Little Boy", Ezekiel 34:12) in his deck.*

6) When playing with the Common Land of Bondage or the Assistance rules variations of the game:

a) When there are no available Lost Souls in any of your opponent's Lands of Bondage, you may announce that you are attempting to rescue a Lost Soul in the common Land of Bondage. The player to your left may play a blocking Evil Character or pass the defense to the next player in line. Once a player has passed the right to block, he cannot later change his mind. If all the players around the table pass in clockwise succession, then the rescue attempt is successful without a battle.

b) When a player asks for assistance, other players may try to help by offering cards from their hands. If the player asking for assistance wants one of the cards offered, then the helping player may give the card to the player who asked for help. The player who is actually in the battle is the one who plays the card. Playing a card makes you the "holder." The "owner" of the card is still the player who actually owns the card. This makes a difference when the effect of the card is determined.

*Example: Giving **False Peace**, **False Wisdom**, or **Cup of Wrath** to assist another player only allows him (since he would be the holder) to look though his draw pile to find a card, look at the rescuer's hand, or choose which Evil Characters fight. Giving **Furnace of God's Wrath** to assist someone would actually allow him to discard one of your Evil Characters in the field of play. **Lies** and **Confusion** are always controlled by the owner of the card.*

FREQUENTLY ASKED QUESTIONS

Some of the same questions about rules have been asked by many people. Some of the most Frequently Asked Questions, or FAQ's, are answered in this chapter. Many other FAQ's are answered by the expanded rules and game examples in this book.

1)   **What happens if there are no remaining cards in a player's draw pile?**

The player continues playing but is not able to draw additional cards. If all players run out of cards and no more rescue attempts can be made, then the game ends. The player with the most Redeemed Souls is the winner. If there are an equal number of Redeemed Souls, then the game is a draw.

2)   **How many rescue attempts may be made per turn?**

Only one rescue attempt may be made per turn. The only exception is that a player may use the **Son of God** card to make a second rescue during the same turn. The **Son of God** card may be played at any time to rescue any Lost Soul from the Land of Bondage, including a Lost Soul in that player's own Land of Bondage.

3)   **If a rescue attempt is announced and my opponent has no Evil Character to block, what happens?**

If no Evil Character is used to block a rescue attempt, the rescue is successful. A player does not have to attempt a rescue or block a rescue attempt if the player believes he cannot win, or if for some other reason, does not believe it is in his best interest to join in battle.

4) **Can the Son of God card be played in reaction to a rescue attempt to deny a Lost Soul to a Hero?**

Yes, if there is a single Lost Soul card in the blocking opponent's Land of Bondage, using the **Son of God** card before the battle is resolved would deny the player from winning a Lost Soul, even if he wins the battle. Using the **Burial** card would have the same effect, but the Lost Soul is discarded rather than redeemed. If there is more than one Lost Soul, the other player makes a rescue from among the remaining Lost Soul cards in that Land of Bondage. When using the **Son of God** card to rescue and remove a Lost Soul during a battle, the **Son of God** card must be played before the battle is completed and the damage delivered, because as soon as a Hero defeats an Evil Character, the battle is won and the Lost Soul becomes a Redeemed Soul out of reach of any instant or enhancement cards.

5) **Is there a limit to the number of Heroes or Evil Characters that may be played per turn?**

There is no limit to the number of cards placed in your territory each turn. However, as stated in the game rules, only one rescue attempt may be made by only one Hero during each turn unless a banding card brings an additional Hero into the battle. Only one Evil Character may block a rescue attempt unless a banding card brings an additional Evil Character into the battle. There is no limit to the number of Heroes or Evil Characters placed into a player's territory during a game or during a turn, except that no two of the same character card may be in the same player's territory or banded together in the field of battle.

6) **Can enhancement cards be played anywhere other than in the Field of Battle?**

Enhancement cards may only be played on character cards in the Field of Battle. Set-aside cards, the exception to this rule, may be played on any character in the field of play. Healing cards may be used on any appropriate character that is about to be discarded as long as they are activated in the field of battle.

7) **How are counters used?**

Counters or markers are used to keep track of the number of turns which a card has been set aside, to track an enhancements from healing cards or set-aside cards, and may be used to differentiate one player's Lost Soul cards or captured Heroes from those of other players. They are also used to score the effects of poisons.

8) **When do special instructions take effect?**

There have been a number of timing questions. Here are some guidelines. Keep track of the order in which cards are being played. When an enhancement card is played which has special instructions (in the form of text over the illustration), its effects are immediate. They take effect before any other card may be played.

*Example: A player is blocking a rescue attempt and plays **Net** to take a Hero prisoner. The Hero is taken prisoner before any other card is played.*

For guidance on the play of the various special instructions, please see the individual card type in the Special Ability Cards section.

9) **How does the Lost Souls card work?**

The **Lost Souls** card counts as a single Lost Soul card for deck building purposes, but counts as two Lost Souls when rescued. The **Lost Souls** card must be rescued twice before either soul can be counted as a Redeemed Soul and placed in a player's Land of Redemption. After the first successful rescue attempt by a player, the card is turned sideways (or the rescuing player's counter is placed on the card). Once this occurs, the card can only be rescued by the same player; unless another player's **Son of God** card can make the rescue, in which case, each player is credited with one rescue.

10) **What are the deck building rules in addition to the rule about Lost Soul cards?**

Each deck may contain only one of each of the lamb icon cards, grim reaper icon cards, and Power Enhancement cards. A deck may only contain one of each special ability card (cards with text printed across the artwork), for each 50 cards in the deck. There is a limit of three of any one card per deck. A player may never have more than one of the same character in his territory at one time. Example: A player may have three **Red Dragon** cards in his deck but never more than one in his territory.

11) **Why is the Christian Martyr card thought to be so tough when there are five healing cards which can reverse its effects?**

Elisha's Bones and **Balm of Gilead** are the only healing cards that can heal a Hero being discarded by **Christian Martyr**. The other healing cards may only save a Hero about to be discarded and since the effects of **Christian Martyr** happen instantaneously, the Hero is already "being" discarded.

12) **May I play an enhancement card on someone else's character?**

No, not unless that ability is on the card (**Repentance**) or you are controlling another player's card, then you may play enhancements on that card. You may play enhancement cards on your own characters which affect other players' characters, but you may not actually play an enhancement card on any character not in your control.

*Example: You may play **Rage** on your own character to pull one of your opponent's characters into the battle with your character and play enhancements on that character card until it is returned after the battle is resolved. But you could not play **Meditation** onto an opponent's **Esther** in order to remove her from a battle to block a rescue attempt.*

13) Are there different cards with the same name in the *Redemption*™ game?

Yes, there are several cards which are different but share the same name. Some cards are variations of other cards (same brigade, different abilities) and some are different cards (different brigade, different or same abilities). There are also printing differences where the wording of text may change, the color of ink may vary, or the artwork may vary. Cards with printing differences are treated as the same card for deck building and playing purposes, but may be treated differently for collecting purposes. There are two **Bow and Arrow** cards and two **Angel Food** cards, but since they are in different brigades, they are treated as different cards for deck building purposes.

14) If one of my human Evil Characters repents, may I then play another of the same Evil Character card into my territory?

Yes, because the repented character is now of a different brigade and is considered to be a different character with the same name.

*Example: If **Goliath** repents and becomes a 10/10 Green Brigade Hero, then you may place a **Goliath** (10/10 Black Brigade Evil Character) into your territory.*

15) Can a return card or capture card cause a set-aside card to be returned to the owners hand?

No, a set-aside card is outside of the field of play. A card must be in the field of play to be affected by any enhancement card.

16) Is it legal to increase the number of Lost Souls needed to win the game?

Yes, see the Optional Advanced Rules. If you do increase the number needed to win, then you may want to increase the number of Lost Soul cards in your decks accordingly or play with more cards in your decks.

17) **If I rescue five of my opponent's Lost Souls, may I keep them when the game is over?**

No, that would be tantamount to gambling. All cards, Lost Souls and captured Heroes included, return to the owner's decks after the game is finished. Only if you make trades with other players should you leave a play session with different cards from those you brought with you. If you want more cards, you can always purchase or trade for them.

18) **Who decides which Lost Soul is rescued in a successful rescue attempt?**

The blocking player chooses which of his or her Lost Souls has been rescued. The only time this affects game play is when the **Lost Souls** card is in the Land of Bondage. The exception is when playing Advanced rule, Rescuers Choice.

19) **Valley of Dry Bones returns "all Heroes from all discard piles to the Field of Play." What if a player winds up with more than one of any Hero? For example, two Elisha cards.**

If a player ends up with more than one of any Hero card in his or her territory after **Valley of Dry Bones** is played, then the duplicate character is discarded because a player may not have more than one of any individual character in one's own territory at any one time.

20) **Can more than one enhancement card of the same title be played on a character?**

Yes. There is no limit to the number of enhancement cards or the number of same name enhancement cards that may be played on a character in the field of battle. Be sure to follow the deck building rules and timing rules concerning enhancement cards.

Example: You may play three Axe cards on Ahab, making him 12/9, but you may not play four, unless you are borrowing from another player in a multiplayer game, because deck building rules require that you have no more than three of any one card in your deck.

21) **How do I determine which character cards are human and which are not? There sometimes seems to be some discrepancy between the artwork and the Scripture reference.**

When playing **Repentance**, use the artwork as a guide for game playing purposes. Do not take this suggestion to be a reinterpretation of Scripture. This is to be understood as a simple visual method for resolving a situation.

22) **Can the Red Brigade enhancement card Healing be played on a character from another brigade?**

The Red Brigade **Healing** card must be activated by playing it on a Red Brigade Hero in the field of battle; however, the healing effect may be played on any other Hero that is about to be discarded. This will occur mostly in banding situations since the Hero, upon which the enhancement is played, must be in the field of battle.

23) **When Cup of Wrath is played, do Evil Characters keep or discard the enhancement cards that have already been placed on them? Can other enhancement cards be added during the battle between the two Evil Characters?**

After **Cup of Wrath** has been played, the original Evil Character keeps its enhancement cards. New enhancement cards may be added to either Evil Character. This makes for some interesting game strategy since the enhancement cards played during this Evil Character-versus-Evil Character battle can affect other characters in the field of play. A good strategy is to select one of your own Evil Characters to fight in order to play an enhancement card of your own or to keep the opposing player from playing one. When one Evil Character loses and is discarded, the enhancement cards on that character are also discarded. Then the initial battle of the rescue attempt continues, if the original Evil Character has survived, with any additional enhancement cards added to the Evil Character remaining until this battle is resolved.

24) **If Cup of Wrath is played and the battle between the two Evil Characters ends in a stalemate, what happens next?**

If the battle between two Evil Characters ends in a stalemate after **Cup of Wrath** has been played, then the two Evil Characters survive the battle. The challenger is returned to its own territory. The Evil Character that was initially blocking the rescue attempt returns to the battle with the Hero making the rescue attempt.

25) **When False Prophecy is played in a banding situation with two non-prophets, are both repelled?**

Yes, both non-prophets are repelled when **False Prophecy** is played against two banded non-prophets. This card repels any Hero that is not a prophet, regardless of how many non-prophet Heroes are in the field of battle, in the same way that a repel brigade card repels any number of Heroes from that brigade. If played against a prophet and non-prophet banded together, then the non-prophet is repelled, but the prophet may deal damage.

Note: It is not always easy to define a prophet. Any Hero, who is a messenger from God, that the Bible calls a prophet should be considered a prophet in the game. Prophets are not exclusive to the Prophets Expansion Set.

26) **Can set-aside characters be brought into play to block a rescue attempt or to band with another player's Hero?**

No. All set-aside characters must be brought back into play during the owner's turn.

OPTIONAL ADVANCED RULES

The following rules add exciting possibilities to the *Redemption*™ card game. They may or may not be used at the discretion of the players. Everyone must agree prior to play if any are to be used.

1) Name-on-name Bonus

An enhancement card is worth double its value when played on a card with a matching name. The names in the title of the card must match. The Scripture verse does not have to refer to the same person as long as the names on the cards are the same. Only the value of the strength and toughness on the enhancement card are doubled. All other effects of the enhancement card remain the same.

*Example: A player making a rescue attempt with **Ruth** (a White 4/4 character) could play **Devotion of Ruth** (a White 1/1 enhancement) to increase the abilities of **Ruth**. In this situation the value of the enhancement card would double, increasing her abilities to 6/6 instead of 5/5. The special ability of the **Devotion of Ruth** will not protect two Heroes from the Gray Brigade.*

2) Assisting a Player

A player may invite other players, using their own decks, to help him make or block a rescue attempt. Then the other players may offer any card(s) to assist the player asking for help. The player in the battle would be the one to actually play a card that he accepted to help out in the battle, making him the holder. All other basic rules of battle still apply. A special ability card, such as a banding card, would still have to be played to allow more than one Evil Character or Hero to be in the field of battle at the same time.

Note: A second character cannot be added to the battle unless a banding card is played. Once the battle is over, all enhancement cards are discarded to each player's respective discard pile. All character cards are returned to the appropriate territory or discarded, if appropriate.

3) The Common Land of Bondage

a) All Lost Soul cards reside together in a single common Land of Bondage. Any time a player draws a Lost Soul card, it goes to the Common Land of Bondage. Any player making a rescue attempt would be blocked by the opponent on his or her left. That opponent has the option of blocking the rescue attempt or passing the option to block to the next opponent and so on.

b) An alternate option would be to have each player place a Lost Soul card in the center of the playing area prior to the beginning of the game. If, on a player's turn, none of the opponents have any Lost Soul cards in their Lands of Bondage, the player may attempt to rescue a Lost Soul from the common Land of Bondage. The opponent to the player's left has the option of blocking the rescue attempt or passing to the next opponent and so on.

Both of these variations become even more interesting if you also play the optional rule, allowing players to help each other.

4) No Doubles in Play

No more than one of each character card may be in the field of play at the same time. In other words, if I put **Jonathan** in play, then none of my opponents can put their **Jonathan** cards in play until my **Jonathan** is discarded. I can have more than one **Jonathan** in my deck, but not in play. This optional rule is more restrictive than what is allowed under the basic rules, but works well in smaller (two or three player) games, especially if playing with basic starter decks.

5) Experience Credit

Characters who successfully win or block a rescue attempt receive a 1/1 counter for each victory in battle. This allows characters to grow with experience.

6) Poisons

Poison and **Bad Figs** count as poison cards. A Hero who has a poison played against him in battle is considered poisoned. If the Hero wins the battle, the effect of the poison remains and the Hero will lose defensive toughness points each round equal to the offensive strength of the poisoning card. If the poisoning enhancement card is removed before the damage is dealt at the end of the battle, then the Hero is not poisoned. A poison can be countered by a card which has the special ability to "*heal*" a Hero or to "*render all poisons harmless.*" If a poison is not countered the Hero continues to lose defensive toughness points until discarded.

The effect of poisons are scored during a player's upkeep phase as follows: on each subsequent turn following a battle in which a Hero has been poisoned, a minus counter for each negative point of toughness is placed on the Hero.

Example: A player plays **Poison** *with* **Goliath**. *The Hero in battle is* **Gideon** *(6/6). After additional enhancement cards are played, the battle is won by* **Gideon**. *However,* **Gideon** *returns to his owner's territory as a poisoned Hero. Since* **Poison** *has two points of strength,* **Gideon's** *toughness will decrease two points at the beginning of* **Gideon's** *owner's next turn. Two negative one (-1) counters are placed on the* **Gideon** *card at that time to record the decrease in toughness (his abilities are at (6/4). In three turns (when his toughness decreases to zero)* **Gideon** *will be discarded unless a card that will "heal" or that "renders all poisons harmless" can be activated on a Hero in battle and its effect directed to* **Gideon**.

7) Rescuer's Choice

Before a player begins a rescue attempt, he must announce which Lost Soul card he is trying to rescue; that is the only Lost Soul card he is eligible to rescue if he wins the rescue attempt. If the Lost Soul has been buried or rescued by another player before the battle is resolved, then the rescuer will not be able to actually bring back that Redeemed Soul, or another one, even if he wins the battle.

8) More Rescues

Many players, especially in multi-player games, have increased the number of Redeemed Souls required to win the game. This alternate rule allows the game to last longer and allows players to play more of their cards during the game. Many players using this option have increased the required number of Redeemed Souls to seven or more. Players may need to increase the number of Lost Soul cards in their decks to compensate when requiring more Redeemed Souls to win the game. *This option can only be used with customized decks.*

THE *REDEMPTION*™ FELLOWSHIP

Redemption™ is not only a wonderful Bible-based game of strategy, but it is also a great way to add a new ministry tool for fellowship and evangelism into any youth group!

In response to the many requests for help in organizing *Redemption*™ tournaments, we are providing information in this section to help civic group leaders, pastors, youth pastors, retailers and anyone else interested in hosting a *Redemption*™ tournament. *Redemption*™ is fun and an edifying activity for youth groups, Sunday school classes, civic groups, and other events.

These guidelines are offered to help you organize a tournament. Please let us know if you have any suggestions about how to improve these guidelines based upon your *Redemption*™ tournament experience.

LEVEL 1 TOURNAMENT SYSTEM

Organizing Suggestions

Choose a location for the tournament that will accommodate the number of players expected for the tournament. Supply an appropriate number of tables and chairs. Publicize the event well ahead of time. Announce it at youth meetings a few weeks before the event, list it in the church bulletin, distribute flyers in your neighborhood and so on.

If you are running a sealed deck tournament you will need to provide enough cards for your players. We recommend contacting your local Christian bookstore, trading card shop, comic book store, gaming store or hobby shop. Inform the store manager that you are organizing a *Redemption*™ tournament. Ask to display one of your flyers at the store. Some store managers may be willing to sell you enough starter decks and booster packs for the tournament at some discount off the normal retail price.

If you are running an open-deck tournament, players will want to bring their custom decks. **Be sure to clearly identify which type of tournament (sealed-deck or open-deck) you are hosting.** Publicity before the tournament should also make it clear to participants whether or not cards will be available at the event or if participants must bring their own decks.

Cactus Game Design, Inc. wants to help support your tournament. Send us a sample flyer, copy of your church bulletin or other promotional material that publicizes your tournament (30 days prior) and Cactus will send you a free promotional card along with a *Redemption*™ Tournament Certificate to give to the winner of your tournament. This promotional card is autographed by the artist and will only be available to players who win a *Redemption*™ Fellowship Tournament. It is not available in stores.

Finally, it is customary for tournament participants to pay for decks and boosters they use in the tournament and to keep those cards after the tournament. If you are supplying the cards at no cost to the participants and do not plan to let them keep the cards, it may be easier and more cost effective to use starter decks without booster packs.

Sealed-deck, Two-player Tournament

1) All basic rules found in the *Redemption*™ rule book apply. The tournament Judge will determine which of the advanced rules will be used. Advanced rules to be used in the tournament should be announced prior to the tournament and be consistent for that event.

2) Tournaments will use a standard ladder-bracket system. Single or double elimination tournaments are both acceptable. A ladder chart should be prepared with players' names clearly printed in their ladder positions.

3) The total number of players in the tournament should be an even factor (i.e., 8, 16, 32, 64 etc.) This avoids problems associated with byes. However, byes can be used if necessary.

4) Tournaments will be presided over by a Judge (usually the host), who may be assisted by as many Assistant Referees as needed. A Judge may be required to interpret rules, interpret a Declaration of Forfeiture, or make any other adjudication as necessary during the tournament. The Judge is also responsible for maintaining the ladder chart. Assistant Referees will aid the Judge by answering rules questions on the floor, and being available to the Judge for any other assistance required. Any Referee's decision is final; however, in necessary cases, the Judge may overrule any decision by an Assistant Referee. The decision of the Judge is always final.

5) A match is defined as the best two out of three games. A player may advance in the tournament bracket after successfully winning one match and reporting this victory to the Judge.

6) Prior to the beginning of the preliminary round, each pair of players should have one starter-deck set and six booster packs on the playing surface. Players flip a coin to determine who plays first. The winner of the coin toss will select the deck he will play, either Deck A or Deck B. The six booster packs are now divided, three to each player. Players may now open their decks and booster packs. At this point each player should have 74 cards (50 from the basic deck and 24 from the three booster packs). Players begin constructing their decks. The two opponents may trade cards to improve their decks. Players should be allowed fifteen minutes to build their decks. All deck construction rules found in the basic game apply in this type of tournament. *Example: a deck of 64 cards must include 9 Lost Soul Cards. Players must play a minimum deck of 50 cards and up to 74 cards.*

Note: The host may need to supply additional Lost Soul cards so that decks meet requirements for deck building.

7) Players may adjust their decks between matches. *Example: A player may play all 74 cards in his deck during his first match. Assuming he wins the match (or is in a double elimination tournament), the player may decide to remove 14 cards from his deck and play the second match with a 60 card deck.*

8) At the conclusion of each game, a player may examine an opponent's cards to verify that the minimum number of Lost Soul cards is contained in the opponent's deck and that no restricted cards are duplicated (i.e., no deck contains two **Angel of the Lord** cards).

Sealed-deck, Multi-player Tournament

All of the rules for Sealed-deck, Two-player tournaments apply with the following additions:

1) Games may consist of three to six players. As much as possible, try to keep the number of players even (i.e. 16 players would be divided into four groups of four).

2) Players should be assigned to their match by some random method such as drawing names. This encourages players to make new friends. It also discourages two friends from ganging up on opponents, especially if playing Advanced Rule #2 that allows players to help each other.

Open-deck, Two-player Tournament

Open deck tournaments by implication mean that players arrive at the tournament with their decks ready to play. All rules under Sealed-deck, Two-player Tournament apply except for rule number six and seven which are replaced by the following:

1) All decks must conform to the deck construction rules found in the basic rule book. In addition, the following restrictions apply:

   a) no deck may contain more than three of any card with the same name in the same brigade (other than Lost Soul cards).

   b) no deck may contain more than one (for each 50 cards in the deck) of any single card that has special instructions written on the card (text over the illustration).

   *Example: A 56-card deck may contain only one **Authority of Christ**, one **Repentance**, etc.... A 100-card deck may contain no more than two **Authority of Christ** cards, two **Repentance** cards and so on. A 150-card deck may contain no more than three of any individual, special ability card.*

   c) no deck may contain more than one of each power enhancement card (multi-color icon) or specialty card (lamb icon or grim reaper icon card).

2) Each deck must contain a minimum of 50 cards including seven Lost Souls. There is no maximum number of cards to a deck as long as it contains the appropriate number of Lost Soul cards. Players are expected to arrive at the tournament with the required number of Lost Soul cards in their decks. The host may want to have some extra Lost Soul cards available in case a player forgets to bring the correct number of Lost Soul cards.

3) Players may use up to three different decks in the same tournament with the following restrictions:

   a) a player must play the same deck for an entire match.

   b) a player may only change decks between matches.

   c) a player may not adjust the contents of any deck once the tournament has begun.

   d) a player found changing the contents of a deck will have the deck removed from tournament play by the Judge or referee and issued a warning. A second instance of deck adjustment by a player will be interpreted by the Judge as a Declaration of Forfeiture.

Open-deck, Multi-player Tournament

The following rules apply as listed in the above sections:

From Sealed-deck, Two-player: rules one, two, three, four, five and eight.

From Sealed-deck, Multi-player: rules one and two.

From Open-deck, Two-player: rules one, two and three.

NEW GAME VARIATIONS

There are five new variations for playing *Redemption*™ included in this section. Three games are solitaire games. *The Castle* can be played as a duel by two players with their own decks, racing to see who can rescue the most Lost Souls before one is trapped without a move. The *Colors and Numbers* game is a variation for children who don't like to be left out of the action but aren't quite ready for the strategy involved in the basic rules. Try these games and let us know what you think about them.

THE SOLITAIRE GAMES

Redemption™ is designed to be a game for two or more players which encourages fellowship as well as discussion about the Bible. Of course, a great deal of strategy is added to the game when all the special ability cards are available to the players who buy the booster packs.

For a game that was designed for two or more players, there are a number of clever ways *Redemption*™ can be played as a solo or solitaire game. In these solo games the Heroes may try to rescue the Lost Soul cards, and the Evil Characters try to capture the Lost Soul cards. Just as in the basic game the winner of a battle is the character which has a greater offensive total than the defense of the opposing character in the field of battle. When there is a mutual destruction situation, both characters are discarded, but the Hero still rescues the Lost Soul.

It is easier to learn these solitaire games (just like the basic game) when you watch someone else play first. If the person you are watching is a kind individual, you may even be allowed to ask questions about his play strategies.

DECK TESTER SOLITAIRE

In this solitaire version of *Redemption*™, players test the relative strength of their own theme decks. Is your Army of God strong enough to overcome an evil force that is just as strong as the one in your own tournament deck? Find out by playing this solitaire game created by David M. Easterling.

Objective

Test your own customized deck against itself. The Army of God tries to rescue Lost Souls and the evil forces try to capture them. The side which wins the most Lost Souls wins the game.

Set-Up

Separate the Lost Soul cards from the rest of the cards, shuffle them and set them face down to the side of the playing area. This will be the Land of Bondage. Separate the Army of God from the evil forces. The lamb icon cards go with the good side and the grim reaper cards go with the evil side. Shuffle both decks separately. Place the "good" draw deck near you as if you were playing a two-player game. Place the "evil" draw deck where your opponent's deck would normally be. (Some players prefer to remove cards such as **Authority of Christ** and **Great Image** from a deck before testing.)

Your field of play will consist of several rows, or lines, for cards. A maximum of four cards may be in any row during a turn. The rows, moving away from the player, are in the following order: good enhancement card line, Hero card line, field of battle, Evil Character card line and the evil enhancement card line.

To set up the starting field of play, draw five cards from the good deck. Place any Heroes in a line in front of you. Place any enhancement cards in the enhancement line behind the Hero line. Then draw five cards from the evil draw deck and place any Evil Characters in a line with the evil enhancement cards in a line behind them. Each side should now have a line of characters facing the field of battle, and behind it a line of enhancements.

Draw Phase

Turn a Lost Soul face up and place it beside the Lost Soul draw deck. This Lost Soul is in the Land of Bondage and is available to be won by the characters. If a special ability card sends a character to the Land of Bondage then that character is placed (face up) beside the Lost Soul in play and is also available to be won by either side. Only turn a Lost Soul face up when the previous Lost Soul has been rescued or discarded. There should only be one Lost Soul card available in the Land of Bondage during each turn, but there may be additional character cards which have been sent there.

Do not draw any additional cards during the first round of play. At the beginning of each subsequent turn draw three cards for each side and decide which cards stay in the game and which ones, if any, will be discarded. A maximum of four enhancement cards can be in any enhancement line at any one time.

A maximum of four characters can be in the character lines at any one time. When you have more than four characters or enhancements for either side after a draw phase, then decide which ones to keep or discard, using the discarding strategies involved in the basic game. You don't have to use all the enhancement cards in every battle.

All cards work as they do in the basic rules. The instant cards also play in the same way as in the basic game. You may place the instant cards in the enhancement line to wait for the best time to play them. When you draw cards and end up with too many in any line, simply discard the weaker ones or the cards which do not match the characters in play. Cards in any line may be replaced by ones which are drawn during the draw phase. You decide when and how long to use the set-aside cards depending upon the best strategy for their forces.

No cards remain in your hand during a Battle Phase. You may not have more than four of any card type in a line when the Battle Phase begins.

Battle Phase

A Hero must make a rescue attempt and an Evil Character must block. Even if there is not a Lost Soul available in the Land of Bondage because it has been buried, a battle must still be initiated in each round. You may add enhancement cards from the enhancement lines to the characters in the same way as in the basic rules. Play continues with the side which is losing playing the next card. Play is limited to the cards on the table. No additional cards are drawn during the Battle Phase, unless a special ability card allows such a play. The good side may only make one rescue attempt during each turn.

If there is no Evil Character in the field of play when the Battle Phase begins, then the good side automatically rescues a Lost Soul from the Land of Bondage and the next draw phase begins a new turn. If there is no Hero in play to make a rescue attempt, then the evil side captures a Lost Soul from the Land of Bondage and the next draw phase is initiated.

Battle Phase Results

When a Hero wins a battle or ties with the Evil Character, then a Lost Soul is rescued from the Land of Bondage and brought over to the good side. When the Evil Character wins a battle or disposes of the rescuing Hero, then a Lost Soul is captured and brought over to the evil side. If a special ability card or an instant card has taken the only Lost Soul card which is face up out of play before a battle is resolved, then there might not be a Lost Soul for the winner to claim. The side which wins the most Lost Souls wins the game. Play continues even when one side runs out of cards in its draw pile.

Why Play the Deck Tester Game?

In this game you try to play the best cards for both sides as if you did not know what each side had. This might seem a little difficult at first, but after a while you really want to see which side is strongest. This game gives you good practice time and builds your playing skills when other players are not around. (Playing your deck against itself might keep you from being embarrassed during a tournament by using a custom deck you made which you thought was unbeatable, but in reality probably couldn't win even if your opponent were actually trying to lose).

The *Deck Tester Solitaire* game can only help you as you customize your play deck. If your Heroes tend to win each game too easily, then you know you need to try to make your evil forces stronger, add some special ability cards, or even change color brigade combinations.

If your Army of God continually takes a pounding at the hands of these evil doers, then you will need to think about adding some different special ability cards or changing color brigade combinations for your good forces. The good thing about this situation is that your defensive capabilities are strong in your deck, but if you cannot actually win five Lost Souls when playing your deck against another player's deck, then let's just say you won't be taking home any promo cards with the artist's signature from your local tournament—unless you purchase one from someone. The bright side is that everyone else at the tournament will be glad to see you and want to play you in the first match.

THE CASTLE

This solitaire game is quite challenging. If you become hooked trying to win it, please do not blame this author, because, at the time of the printing of this book, he has only won once himself.

The Castle game is played by combining most of the A and B starter decks. Remove the grim reaper cards, Black Brigade, and the Pale Green Brigade. Also remove one Green Brigade character, one evil Gold Brigade character, and one Brown character card. Remove one Green, one Purple, and one Red enhancement card. Remove one Lost Soul. Set these cards aside because you will not play with them in this game.

You should now have 85 cards to play with in this game. The object of this game is to rescue all 13 Lost Souls from the five castle towers in which they are imprisoned.

Shuffle all 85 cards together. Then deal them face down into five stacks of 17 cards each. Each stack represents a castle tower with Lost Souls scattered randomly within. Place four of the stacks in a square with the fifth stack in the middle of the others.

Turn over the top card of each castle stack and place it on top of the tower stack. Next to each castle tower is a space we will call the tower gate. Whenever a card is played from the top of a tower to a gate, the next card in the tower is turned over. A character card may be placed at any tower gate. You will try to obtain three more cards of the same color brigade to go with that character. However, the 14 rainbow cards are wild cards and may be played with any color brigade. Wild cards may also be used as character cards to begin a brigade team at a gate, but a card of that color must immediately be placed with that wild card when it is used in such a way.

When four of the same color are at one of the outside gates they may escort a Lost Soul from the castle to safety. When a Lost Soul is turned over on top of a tower it may join any of the brigades at a tower gate. Only one Lost Soul may join each brigade. The brigade at the central tower gate may only leave the castle by moving to an empty corner gate first.

In this game all cards are basically good and are used to rescue Lost Souls. Notwithstanding this, treat the different Gold Brigade cards as two different brigades which don't work together. Try to move cards out of the towers as evenly as possible. The trick to the game is not leaving yourself without a place to play. With ten colors and only five gates to send brigades to, you may find yourself cut off without a play unless you plan carefully. If you have a completed color brigade, with no Lost Soul available to rescue, and you can't move any other cards, you may allow that color brigade to leave the castle without saving a Lost Soul. This will make room for a new color brigade to start at that empty tower gate and allow another tower card to be revealed.

If you need to make this game easier let a color brigade of only three cards rescue a Lost Soul. This game will also be easier if you establish a certain number of Lost Soul cards that must be rescued to win the game. Try starting by rescuing seven Lost Souls to win, and work your way up to all 13 as you learn the strategy.

Threes

Try this fast-paced solitaire game from R. Craig Haines.

Game Play

You may use an A or B deck, both decks together, or even your own customized deck. Remove all the Lost Soul cards from the deck and place them
face up in a single pile. The object is for your Heroes to rescue more Lost Soul
cards than the Evil Characters can capture. You go through your deck three
times keeping track of how many Lost Souls each side has won. (If you run out
of Lost Soul cards, write down the score and use them again.)

Set-Up

Your field of play will consist of several rows or lines for cards. The four rows,
moving away from the player, are in the following order: good enhancement
cards line, good character space, Evil Character space, and the evil enhancement
cards line. A maximum of one character card may be in either of the character
rows at one time. A maximum of three enhancement cards may be in any
enhancement card row during a turn.

Actual game play is simple and uses the same basic rules as a two player game.
First divide your playing area into two sides. One side is for the evil forces and
the other is for the Army of God. Place the Lost Souls pile in the middle near
the side of the playing field. Holding the deck of cards (minus the Lost Soul
cards lying faceup on the table), turn the cards over one at a time. These are the
possible outcomes:

Drawing a Hero

When you draw a Hero, place the card face up on the table on the good side. If
there is already a Hero lying on the table when you draw another Hero you
may keep either one and discard the other. There is to be only one Hero in the
playing field at a time. The Hero may use any of the good enhancement cards
that are in the good enhancement row during a Battle Challenge as they were
played from your hand following the basic game rules.

Drawing an Enhancement Card

When an enhancement card is drawn, either for the Army of God or the evil forces, it is placed on the table in a horizontal row on the appropriate side until a maximum of three enhancement cards per side are lying face up. You must lay down enhancement cards as they are drawn. When you draw an enhancement card of either side and there are already three enhancement cards in that enhancement row, the new card is simply discarded. Only when an enhancement card is played with a character card, creating a space for a new one, can a new enhancement card drawn from the deck be placed in the enhancement row.

Drawing an Evil Character

When an Evil Character is drawn from the deck, a battle will result for a Lost Soul if a Hero is also in the field of play. If there is no Hero lying on the table, then continue drawing until one comes up and send it to the field of battle. During a battle the Evil Character may use any of the enhancement cards that are already in the evil enhancement card row.

An Evil Character does not stay in the field of play after a battle challenge. Win or lose, the Evil Character and any enhancement cards used are discarded at the end of the battle.

Battle

When there is a Hero and an Evil Character in the field of battle, then a battle occurs with the results following the basic rules for combat.

It is possible that there might not be any enhancement cards at all in the enhancement row to help out the characters or that none of the enhancement colors will match the characters. It depends on the order in which the cards are drawn. If no special ability cards are played which effectively take one of the characters out of the battle, compute the offensive and defensive scores as in normal play and whoever wins the battle wins the Lost Soul card which is placed on the appropriate side of the Lost Soul pile. Any enhancement cards that were used are discarded, and if the good character is defeated, that card is also discarded.

Game play continues in this way until you have played through your deck three times. Shuffle the play deck each time you have gone through it before you begin a new round. After three rounds determine which side has won the most Lost Soul cards.

Specialty Cards

Most specialty cards can be played as in a two-player game. But because of the diversity of special ability cards such as **Son of God**, **Christian Martyr**, and **Ezekiel's Stick**, some won't fit into the structure of this solitaire game. For best game play, discard the following types of cards: lamb, grim reaper, set-aside, banding, and any cards that do something outside of the field of battle. In addition, when a card, such as **Net** or **Stocks**, has captured a Hero, add that Hero to the Lost Soul pile for the rest of the game. Then discard that special ability card for the remainder of that game, or you may end up with six to nine Heroes in the Lost Soul pile and have no one left to make rescues.

THE MULTI-PLAYER GAMES

COLORS AND NUMBERS

This variation was created by David Easterling so that children who could not quite understand the basic game could still have a game to play with *Redemption*™ cards.

Objective

This game is for two or more players. Players may play with an A deck and B deck or left-over common cards. Players should decide how many cards with which to play, as well as the maximum number of cards from each color to use. Once again, as with all *Redemption*™ games, the object is to rescue Lost Souls. Each player places the same number of Lost Soul cards, face down, by his draw piles. Players who win each Battle Challenge rescue one of their own Lost Soul cards. The player who first rescues all of his or her own Lost Souls wins the game.

Set-up

All players deal themselves eight cards. Four cards are placed face up in front of each player and the other four cards are held in their hands. Players choose which cards to place on the table and which cards to hold in their hands. At the beginning of each turn all players draw four cards. Players must then decide which cards to play on the table and which cards to hold in their hands before the Battle Challenge phase. Players must have four cards in their waiting line before a Battle Challenge Phase. If a player should have fewer than four cards before going into a Battle Challenge, then those cards all need to be on the table. If a player has more than eight cards after a draw phase, then the extra cards must be discarded before any other action occurs. Cards may go from a player's hand to the face-up row in the play area. Once a card is played face-up it may not go back to a player's hand.

Battle Challenge

When all players have drawn and discarded as necessary, the Battle Challenge phase happens. Taking turns, a different player places the first character in the field of battle each round. During the Battle Challenge, players take turns adding a card of the same color to their color brigade in the field of Battle until one player decides not to play anymore. The first card played by each player must be a character card. Additional cards may be either character, enhancement, power enhancement or specialty cards. Any of the players may also choose to pass that round; someone who passes cannot win a Lost Soul and therefore makes it easier for another player to win. The special abilities of cards are ignored for this game.

The player who wins the Battle Challenge may turn one Lost Soul card over for that turn. All players who are tied for a win may turn over a Lost Soul for that turn.

Winning a Battle Challenge

For younger children you may play with the colors. The one who can play the most cards of the same color in the field of battle wins the Lost Soul during that turn. Power enhancement and specialty cards may be played as any color. The lamb and grim reaper cards can also be used to represent a character of any color to begin a color brigade at the beginning of a Battle Phase if the player doesn't have a Character card in the color he or she wants to play. Each player plays one card at a time until the other players cannot or choose not to play any more. All cards from all sides that were actually played in the field of battle are discarded at the end of each round.

Older children may play for the numbers. Whoever can build the highest offensive score (from cards of one color played in the field of battle) wins the Lost Soul that turn. The offensive number is the first number in the top left corner of a card. When playing this way, take out any cards which do not have numbers in the color square before the game begins. This game variation is not only fun for children, but also helps to build math skills.

Winning the Game

The player who turns over all of his or her Lost Soul cards first wins the game. If no one turns over all the Lost Souls by the time all the players have run out of cards in their draw piles, and no more moves can be made, the game is over and whoever has the most Lost Souls turned face up wins the game. It is permissible for the game to end in a draw.

FREESTYLE

Freestyle is a wild game of strong characters and powerful enhancement cards that most players will enjoy. It is quick to learn if you already know the basic and optional advanced rules for *Redemption*™. The game moves fast because you have an opportunity to play many enhancement cards. Battles which are decided by the numbers regularly go as high as 20/20. You will find some new twists in the strategy needed to play this game.

Freestyle may be played by two or more players. You might even want to try this game variation on Threes or Deck Tester solitaire. You may play with the A and B starter decks, your customized deck, or a deck that you have customized specifically for the **Freestyle** variation game. A *Freestyle* customized deck of 100 cards is recommended.

Freestyle has all of the same basic rules as *Redemption*™ with the following exceptions:

A) Any Hero enhancement card of any color brigade may be played on any Hero in the field of battle.

B) Any Hero enhancement card played on a Hero of the same color brigade will be permanent, and does not need to be discarded until the Hero is discarded.

C) Any evil enhancement card of any color brigade may be played on any Evil Character in the field of battle.

D) Any evil enhancement card played on an Evil Character of the same color brigade will be permanent, and does not need to be discarded until the Evil Character is discarded.

E) Enhancement cards of a different color brigade from the character on which it is played must be discarded at the end of the turn.

F) Special abilities on any enhancement card will only happen once, and only during the turn in which the card is initially played.

G) Cards that heal may be played on any character of the same color brigade and remain for the rest of the game. Cards that heal may also be played on characters from other color brigades, but must be discarded at the end of the turn.

H) Multi-colored enhancements are permanent on any color and may be played on any character in the field of play, in or out of the field of battle.

I) The following advanced optional rules are standard and always apply.
   1. Name-on-name Bonus
   2. Assisting a Player
   3. Experience Credit
   4. Poisons

J) Other advanced optional rules may be introduced into the *Freestyle* game if all players agree prior to the beginning of the game.

Your deck building strategy for *Freestyle* will be somewhat different from that for the standard *Redemption*™ game. This is your opportunity to use the best special ability cards from color brigades you don't usually play. It is still a good strategy to only use three or four main brigades in your deck because the same color enhancements permanently remain on the character. When you revise your deck for a Freestyle game, follow the basic deck building rules that pertain to the number of Lost Souls, specialty cards, and special ability cards in your deck.

When a battle gets down to the numbers, if no one plays special ability winners or stoppers, then the numbers will really add up. Don't be surprised if you find yourself with a 20/26 **Esther** battling a 24/21 **Goliath**.

One temptation of this game is to play all of your enhancement cards in one battle. Resist or you may find yourself in the next battle with only a couple of enhancement cards facing an opponent who exercised self-control during the last encounter.

THE COLLECTOR'S CORNER

The Cards in alphabetical order, sorted by Type, Rarity, and Set.

Type
H	=	Hero
HE	=	Hero Enhancement
EC	=	Evil Character
EE	=	Evil Enhancement
L	=	Lamb icon
GR	=	Grim Reaper icon
LS	=	Lost Soul

Rarity	=	Booster Pack distribution
C	=	Common
U	=	Uncommon
R	=	Rare

Set
Lp	=	Limited Promotion
L	=	Limited Booster Pack
A	=	Limited A Deck
B	=	Limited B Deck
u	=	Unlimited Booster Pack
a	=	Unlimited A Deck
b	=	Unlimited B Deck
P	=	Prophets Expansion Set

Name	Type	Color	Rarity	Set
Aaron's Rod	HE	Green	R	L,A,U,a
Abaddon the Destroyer	EC	Black	R	L,U
Abandonment	EE	Gold	R	L,U
Abihu	EC	Gray	U	L,U
Adino	H	Red	U	L,U
Agabus	H	Green	U	P
Ahab	EC	Brown	U	L,B,U,b
Ahaziah	EC	Brown	U	P
Alertness	HE	Purple	C	L,U
Amos	H	Green	U	P
Angel Food	HE	White	C	L,B,U,b
Angel Food	HE	Gold	–	Lp
Angel of the Lord	L		–	A,B,a,b
Anna	H	Blue	C	P
Antidote	HE	White		L,U
Arrow of Deliverance	HE	Red	C	P
Asahel	H	Red	U	L,U
Ashtaroth Worship*	EE	Pale Green	C	P
Astrologers	EC	Gold	U	P
Authority of Christ	HE	Purple	R	L,U
Axe	EE	Brown	C	L,B,U,b
Baal Worship	EE	Crimson	C	P
Bad Figs	EE	Brown	C	P
Baggage	HE	Red	R	P
Balaam	EC	Gray	U	P
Balm of Gilead	HE	Blue	R	L,B,U,b
Banner	HE	White	C	L,B,U,b
Banner of Love	HE	Green	C	L,U
Barnabas	H	Blue	U	L,B,U,b
Battle Axe	HE	Red	C	L,U
Beast from the Earth	EC	Brown	R	L,U
Beast from the Sea	EC	Pale Green	R	L,U
Belshazzar	EC	Crimson	C	P
Boils	EE	Brown	C	L,B,U,b
Bow And Arrow	EE	Gray	C	L,A,a
Bow and Arrow	HE	Red	U	L,A,U,a
Brass Serpent	HE	Gold	R	L,U
Bravery of David	HE	Red	C	L,U

Name	Type	Color	Rarity	Set
Bread of Life	HE	Green	R	L,U
Breastplate of Righteousness	HE	Multi	—	A,B,a,b
Buckler	HE	Red	C	L,U
Burial	GR		–	Lp,b
Cage	EE	Brown	R	L,U
Chains	EE	Gray	R	L,A,U, a
Chaldeans	EC	Gray	U	P
Chariots of Iron	EE	Crimson	C	L,B,U,b
Chariots of the Sun	EE	Pale Green	C	L,U
Charred Vine	HE	White	R	P
Chastisement of the Lord	HE	Blue	R	L,U
Christian Martyr	GR		–	A,B,a
Christian Soldier	H	Red	U	L,A,U,a
Clemency of David	HE	Green	R	L,A,U,a
Coat of Mail	HE	Red	C	L,U
Commitment of Paul	HE	Green	C	L,U
Compassion of Jeremiah	HE	White	R	L,U
Confusion	EE	Pale Green	R	P
Cornelius	H	Green	U	L,A,U,a
Courage	HE	Blue	U	L,B,U
Courage of Esther	HE	Purple	C	L,U
Covenant with Death	EE	Crimson	C	P
Cruelty	EE	Brown	R	L,U
Cup of Wrath	HE	Blue	R	P
Damsel with Spirit of Divination	EC	Black	U	P
Daniel	H	White	U	P
Darkness	EE	Pale Green	R	L,A,U,a
David's Sling	HE	Red	U	L,U
David's Staff	HE	Red	U	L,A,U,a
Deborah	H	Gold	U	L,A,U,a
Dedication of Samuel	HE	Gold	C	L,U
Delilah	EC	Brown	R	L,U
Den of Robbers	EE	Gold	R	P
Determination of Nehemiah	HE	Green	C	L,U

Name	Type	Color	Rarity	Set
Devotion of Ruth	HE	White	R	L,B,U,b
Discord	EE	Crimson	C	L,U
Doeg	EC	Pale Green	U	L,A,U,a
Drawn Sword	HE	Blue	C	P
Dungeon of Malchiah	EE	Brown	R	P
Ehud's Dagger	HE	Red	C	L,U
Elisha	H	Purple	U	P
Elisha's Bones	HE	Purple	R	P
Enchanter	EC	Brown	U	P
Endurance	HE	Green	C	L,U
Esther	H	Purple	U	L,B,U,b
Evil	EE	Pale Green	C	L,U
Ezekiel	H	Purple	U	P
Ezekiel's Stick	HE	Purple	R	L,B,U
Faith	HE	Blue	U	L,B,U,b
Faith of Abraham	HE	Blue	C	L,U
Faithful Servant	H	Green	U	L,A,U,a
Faithfulness of Luke	HE	Gold	C	L,U
False Dreams	EE	Gray	R	P
False Peace	EE	Gray	R	P
False Prophesy	EE	Gray	R	P
False Prophets	EC	Gray	R	P
False Shepherds	EC	Gray	U	L,A,U,a
False Teachers	EC	Gray	U	L,A,U,a
False Wisdom	EE	Gray	C	P
Fearlessness of Joshua	HE	Gold	C	L,U
Fiery Darts	EE	Crimson	C	L,B,U,b
Filthy Garments	EE	Pale Green	U	P
First Figs	EE	Crimson	C	P
Five Smooth Stones	HE	Red	C	L,U
Floating Ax Head	HE	White	C	P
Forcefulness of Isaiah	HE	Green	C	L,U
Forest Fire	HE	Red	U	P
Forgiveness of Joseph	HE	White	C	L,U
Four Horns	EE	Crimson	U	P
Frog Demons	EC	Pale Green	R	L,U
Furnace of God's Wrath	HE	Gold	R	P
Gad	H	Red	U	P

Name	Type	Color	Rarity	Set
Gentleness	HE	Purple	C	L,U
Gideon	H	Gold	U	L,A,U,a
Goat with Horn	EE	Black	C	P
Golden Lamp Stand	HE	Green	C	P
Goliath	EC	Black	R	L,U
Goliath's Spear	EE	Black	C	L,U
Goodness	HE	Red	C	L,U
Great Image	EE	Crimson	R	P
Grief	EE	Gold	C	L,A,U,a
Habakkuk	H	Purple	U	P
Haman	EC	Brown	U	L,B,U,b
Hammer of God	HE	Gold	C	P
Hannah	H	Blue	U	L,U
Hard-hearted Religious Leaders	EC	Gray	C	L,U
Hate	EE	Black	R	L,U
Healing	HE	Red	R	L,U
Helmet of Brass	HE	Red	U	L,A,U,a
Helmet of Salvation	HE	Multi	–	A,B,a,b
Herodias	EC	Gold	U	L,A,U,a
Highway	HE	Gold	U	P
Hinds' Feet	HE	Purple	C	P
Hope	HE	Red	C	L,U
Hosea	H	Purple	U	P
Huldah	H	Gold	U	P
Humility of Moses	HE	Gold	C	L,A,U,a
Hunger	EE	Black	R	P
Hushai	H	Red	U	L,A,U,a
Ignorance	EE	Brown	U	P
Image of Jealousy	EE	Brown	C	P
Iron Pan	HE	Blue	U	P
Isaiah	H	Green	U	P
Jaazaniah	EC	Gold	U	L,U
Jeremiah	H	White	U	P
Jezebel	EC	Crimson	U	L,B,U,b
Joab	H	Red	R	L,U
John	H	Purple	U	P
John the Baptist	H	White	U	P

Name	Type	Color	Rarity	Set
Jonah	H	Blue	U	P
Jonathan	H	Purple	U	L,B,U,b
Joy	HE	Purple	C	L,U
Judas Iscariot	EC	Crimson	U	L,B,U,b
Kindness	HE	Gold	R	L,U
Lance	EE	Pale Green	C	L,A,U,a
Large Tree	EE	Pale Green	R	P
Leaves for Healing	HE	Purple	R	L,U
Lies	EE	Gold	U	P
Lion Dwelling with the Calf	HE	White	R	P
Live Coal	HE	Green	C	P
Locusts from the Pit	EC	Black	R	L,B,U,b
Long-suffering of John	HE	Purple	C	L,U
Lost Soul Beggar in White – Ezekiel 36:19	LS		–	Lp,a,b
Lost Soul Blind Man – Job 33:27-28	LS		–	A,B,a,b
Lost Soul Green Hand – Ephesians 5:14	LS		–	A,B,a,b
Lost Soul Man at Door – Luke 13:25	LS		R	L,U
Lost Soul Man with Dagger – II Tim. 3:6-7	LS		–	A,B,a,b
Lost Soul Prisoner – Isaiah 42:7	LS		R	L,U
Lost Soul Old Widow – I Kings 17:12	LS		U	L,A,B,U
Lost Soul Seated Beggar – Luke 15:6	LS		—	A,B,a,b
Lost Soul Little Boy – Ezekiel 34:12	LS		U	L,A,B,U,a,b
Lost Soul Woman in Black – II Tim. 2:26	LS		U	L,A,B,U,a,b
Lost Souls Two Women – Proverbs 22:14	LS		R	L,U
Love	HE	Blue	C	L,U
Loyalty of Jonathan	HE	Purple	C	L,B,U,b

Name	Type	Color	Rarity	Set
Malachi	H	Red	U	P
Manasseh	EC	Black	U	P
Manasseh's Altar	EE	Black	C	P
Mark	H	Blue	U	L,B,U,b
Mary	H	White	R	Lp,L,B,U,b
Measuring Line	HE	Blue	C	P
Meditation	HE	Purple	R	Lp,U,b
Meekness of Isaac	HE	White	R	L,U
Mercy of James	HE	Purple	C	L,B,U,b
Mighty Warrior	H	Red	U	Lp,L,A,U,a
Miriam	H	Green	U	L,A,U,a
Molech Worship	EE	Gray	R	P
Molten Calf Worship	EE	Brown	U	P
Moses	H	Gold	R	P
Mountain of God	HE	White	C	P
Nebuchadnezzar	EC	Crimson	U	P
Net	EE	Black	R	L,B,U,b
Obedience of Noah	HE	Blue	R	Lp,L,B,U,b
Ointment	HE	Green	U	L,A,U,a
Othniel	H	Gold	U	L,A,U,a
Paintings of Abominations	EE	Gold	U	P
Patience	HE	Green	C	L,U
Patience of Job	HE	Blue	R	L,U
Paul's Girdle	EE	Brown	C	P
Peace	HE	Gold	R	L,A,U,a
Pharaoh	EC	Gold	U	L,A,U,a
Philip's Daughters	H	White	C	P
Pillar of a Cloud	HE	Multi	–	A,B,b
Plague of Flies	HE	Gold	R	Lp,U
Poison	EE	Black	C	L,B,U,b
Potter and the Clay	HE	Red	U	P
Prayer and Fasting	HE	Gold	R	L,A,U,a
Prince of Persia	EC	Pale Green	R	P
Prophets of Baal	EC	Crimson	U	P
Prophets of Samaria	EC	Black	U	P
Purity of Enoch	HE	White	C	L,B,U,b
Rage	EE	Pale Green	R	L,U

Name	Type	Color	Rarity	Set
Ram with Two Horns	EE	Gold	R	P
Razor	HE	Blue	C	P
Rebekah	H	Blue	U	L,U
Red Dragon	EC	Crimson	R	L,U
Repentance	HE	Green	R	L,U
River Flowing from Temple	HE	Purple	R	P
Rod of Iron	HE	Blue	C	L,U
Ruth	H	White	U	L,B,U,b
Salome	EC	Crimson	U	L,B,U,b
Samson	H	Gold	R	L,U
Samuel	H	Gold	U	L,A,U,a
Shamgar	H	Red	U	L,U
Shemaiah	EC	Black	U	P
Shield of Faith	HE	Multi	–	A,B,a,b
Shimei	EC	Brown	U	L,B,U,b
Shoes of Peace	HE	Multi	–	Lp,a
Silas	H	Blue	U	L,B,U,b
Simeon	H	Gold	U	P
Sleep	HE	White	R	L,U
Snare	EE	Gray	R	L,U
Son of God	L		–	A,B,a,b
Sound the Alarm	HE	Red	R	L,A,U,a
Speed	HE	Purple	R	L,U
Steadfastness of Peter	HE	Red	C	L,A,U,a
Stillness	HE	Blue	–	Lp,b
Stocks	EE	Pale Green	R	L,U
Stone Cut without Hands	HE	Green	U	P
Stone of Thebez	EE	Gold	C	L,A,U,a
Stone Throwers	EC	Crimson	U	L,B,U,b
Strange Vine	EE	Pale Green	C	P
Strength	HE	Blue	C	L,B,U,b
Submissiveness of Mary	HE	White	R	L,B,U,b.
Sun Worship	EE	Multi	R	P
Sword of the Spirit	HE	Multi	–	A,B,a,b
Taskmaster	EC	Gold	U	L,A,U,a
Temperance	HE	Red	U	L,U

Name	Type	Color	Rarity	Set
The Branch	HE	Purple	U	P
The False Prophet	EC	Gray	R	P
The Flying Scroll	EE	Gold	C	P
The Girdle	EE	Gold	C	P
The Vineyard	HE	Purple	R	P
The Watchman	H	Green	U	P
Torn Mantle	EE	Pale Green	R	P
Treachery	EE	Crimson	C	L,B,U,b
Truthfulness of Nathan	HE	Blue	C	L,U
Two Olive Branches	HE	Gold	R	P
Uriah	H	Red	U	L,A,U,a
Users of Curious Arts	EC	Gold	U	P
Vain Philosophy	EE	Crimson	R	L,U
Vain Vision	EE	Black	U	P
Valley of Dry Bones	HE	Green	R	P
Wall of Fire	HE	White	U	P
Weeping for Tammuz	EE	Crimson	C	P
Wheel within a Wheel	HE	Red	R	P
Whore of Babylon	EC	Crimson	R	L,U
Wildness	EE	Gray	R	L,U
Wisdom	HE	Gold	U	L,A,U,a
Witch of Endor	EC	Pale Green	R	P
Wizards	EC	Pale Green	U	P
Woman in the Ephah	EE	Black	C	P
Workers with Familiar Spirits	EC	Pale Green	U	P
Yoke of Iron	EE	Black	R	P
Zechariah	H	Green	C	P
Zephaniah	H	Blue	C	P

* There are two illustrations for Ashtaroth Worship, one by Bill Hodgson and one by Joe Boulden. This is considered to be one card for game play and deck building.

PROMOTIONAL CARDS

There have been ten promotional cards printed. They are listed below. Four of the cards are considered variations of standard cards, as they vary in either strength and toughness or special abilities.

Mary is a 6/6 Hero from the White Brigade, but her strength and toughness increase 3/3 if played during the month of December.

Obedience of Noah loses the standard special ability but increases in strength and toughness to 3/3.

Mighty Warrior has increased strength and toughness to 6/6 as opposed to the standard 4/4.

Angel Food is considered a separate card. Although the 3/3 enhancement is the same for the standard and promotional card, the color brigade is different. The **Angel Food** promotional card is a part of the Gold Brigade, while the standard **Angel Food** card is part of the White Brigade. The other six promotional cards, listed below, have subsequently been printed as standard cards in the Unlimited Edition.

Name	Type	Color	Promotion
Burial	GR		General promotion
Lost Soul Beggar in White – Ezekiel 36:19	LS		General Promotion
Meditation	HE	Purple	General Promotion
Plague of Flies	HE	Gold	General Promotion
Stillness	HE	Blue	General Promotion
Shoes of Peace	HE	Multi	Origins Covention, 1995

FUTURE EXPANSION SETS

The next expansion set for *Redemption*™ will be **Women of the Bible**. This set will introduce a new type of card, Site cards. Normally, Lost Soul cards are held in the Land of Bondage at large. Site cards represent specific locations within the Land of Bondage, such as Babylon, Egypt, and Kir. A Hero must have "access" to a Site in order to rescue a Lost Soul being held prisoner there.

Other upcoming expansion sets include:

The Judges

The Warriors

The Priests

The Apostles

The Prophets, Volume II

The Masterpiece Series

The Masterpiece Series will use classic religious art for card illustrations.

SUGGESTED RETAIL PRICE SHEET

Product	Mfg. Stock #	Price (Suggested Retail)	ISBN #
Limited Edition of 162 game cards			
01) Double Deck Starter Deck (LE)	Now only available in the Gift Set		
02) Starter Deck Display Box (LE)	SOLD OUT		
03) Booster Pack (LE)	CGD201	$1.50	0-9647082-2-1
04) Booster Pack Display Box (LE)	CGD2011	$67.50	0-9647082-3-X
Revised Edition of 168 game cards			
05) Double Deck Starter Deck (R)	CGD102	$9.95	0-9647082-4-8
06) Starter Deck Display Box (R)	CGD1021	$59.70	0-9647082-5-6
07) Booster Pack (R)	CGD202	$1.50	0-9647082-6-4
08) Booster Display (R)	CGD2021	$67.50	0-9647082-7-2
THE PROPHETS Limited Edition expansion set of 105 new, different game cards in booster packs only.			
09) Prophets Booster Pack	CGD203	$1.50	0-9647082-8-0
10) Prophets Booster Display Box	CGD2031	$67.50	0-9647082-9-9
Combo Displays			
11) System Combo Display	CGD4011	$69.80	1-889055-01-8
12) System w/Prophets Combo Display	CGD4021	$69.80	1-889055-02-6
13) Booster Combo Display	CGD4031	$67.50	1-889055-03-4
Gift Set			
14) Gift Set	CGD501	$19.95	1-889055-00-X
Player's Guide			
15) Player's Guide	CGD601	$9.95	1-889055-04-2

PRODUCT FORMAT

Double Deck Starter Deck: 100 cards (50 per deck) in special card mixes ready for play by two players, packaged in two four-color tuckboxes with rule book and over-shrink-wrapped.

Starter Deck Display Box: Six double decks packaged in a four-color display box and over-shrink-wrapped.

Booster Pack: Eight game cards randomly mixed including one rare, three uncommon and four common cards packaged in four-color foil packs.

Booster Display Box: 45 booster packs packaged in a four-color display box and over-shrink-wrapped.

System Combo Display: Four starter deck sets and 20 booster packs. Note: System with PROPHETS substitutes with ten PROPHETS booster packs.

Booster Combo Display: Contains 15 limited edition boosters, 15 unlimited edition boosters, and 15 PROPHETS boosters.

Gift Set: Contains one double starter deck with rule book, a card list of all *Redemption*™ cards printed through June 1996, six booster packs and a special, promotional card only sold in the Gift Set.

Players Guide: Soft cover...strategy, tactics and answers.

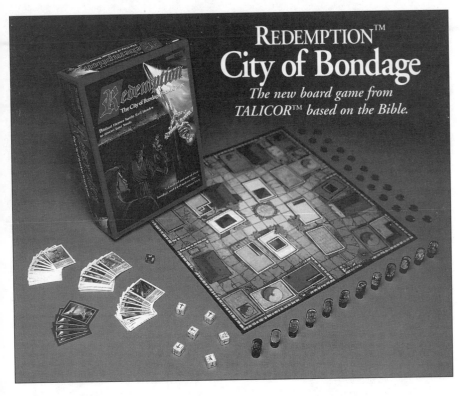

PLAYER'S SURVEY

Please give us your comments on the *Redemption*™ trading card game.

Please rate the following (please circle)
1 = poor, 5 = excellent

1 2 3 4 5   Clarity

1 2 3 4 5   Playability

1 2 3 4 5   Artwork

1 2 3 4 5   Treatment of Topic

Would you recommend this game to a friend?
(please circle):   Yes   No

What, if anything, do you like about the game? _____

_____

_____

_____

What, if anything, do you dislike about the game? _____

_____

_____

_____

How can we improve this game? _____

_____

_____

_____

Participation in this survey is voluntary and the respondent waives any and all rights to any suggestions for improvements or changes. Everyone who responds with a completed survey will receive a promotion card from **Cactus Game Design, Inc.**

Permission granted to photocopy this page to submit survey response.
Facsimile responses may be made to (757) 366 9913.
E-Mail responses may be made to CactusRob@aol.com

INDEX

MY PERSONAL DECK

1. _____   26. _____

2. _____   27. _____

3. _____   28. _____

4. _____   29. _____

5. _____   30. _____

6. _____   31. _____

7. _____   32. _____

8. _____   33. _____

9. _____   34. _____

10. _____   35. _____

11. _____   36. _____

12. _____   37. _____

13. _____   38 _____

14. _____   39. _____

15. _____   40. _____

16. _____   41. _____

17. _____   42. _____

18. _____   43. _____

19. _____   44. _____

20. _____   45. _____

21. _____   46. _____

22. _____   47. _____

23. _____   48. _____

24. _____   49. _____

25. _____   50. _____

51. _____   76. _____

52. _____   77. _____

53. _____   78. _____

54. _____   79. _____

55. _____   80. _____

56. _____   81. _____

57. _____   82. _____

58. _____   83. _____

59. _____   84. _____

60. _____   85. _____

61. _____   86. _____

62. _____   87. _____

63. _____   88. _____

64. _____   89. _____

65. _____   90. _____

66. _____   91. _____

67. _____   92. _____

68. _____   93. _____

69. _____   94. _____

70. _____   95. _____

71. _____   96. _____

72. _____   97. _____

73. _____   98. _____

74. _____   99. _____

75. _____   100. _____